Nature in Story and Verse..

A Dear Little Girl was Looking for Leaves

NATURE

IN STORY AND VERSE

For the Kindergarten School and Home

By
KITTIE BALDWIN JAQUES
Graduate of
St. Louis Kindergarten Training School

Chicago
The Henneberry Company
1912

 241

$1.00

*Lovingly Dedicated
to my Two Children*
whose happy childhood has
been the inspiration for these
Stories and Verses

THEN Nature, the good old Nurse,
  Took the young child on her knee,
And whispered: "Here is a story book
  Thy Father has written for thee."

Selected

I find Earth not gray, but rosy—
  Heaven not grim, but fair of hue.
Do I stoop? I pluck a posy.
  Do I stand and stare? All's blue.

Robert Browning

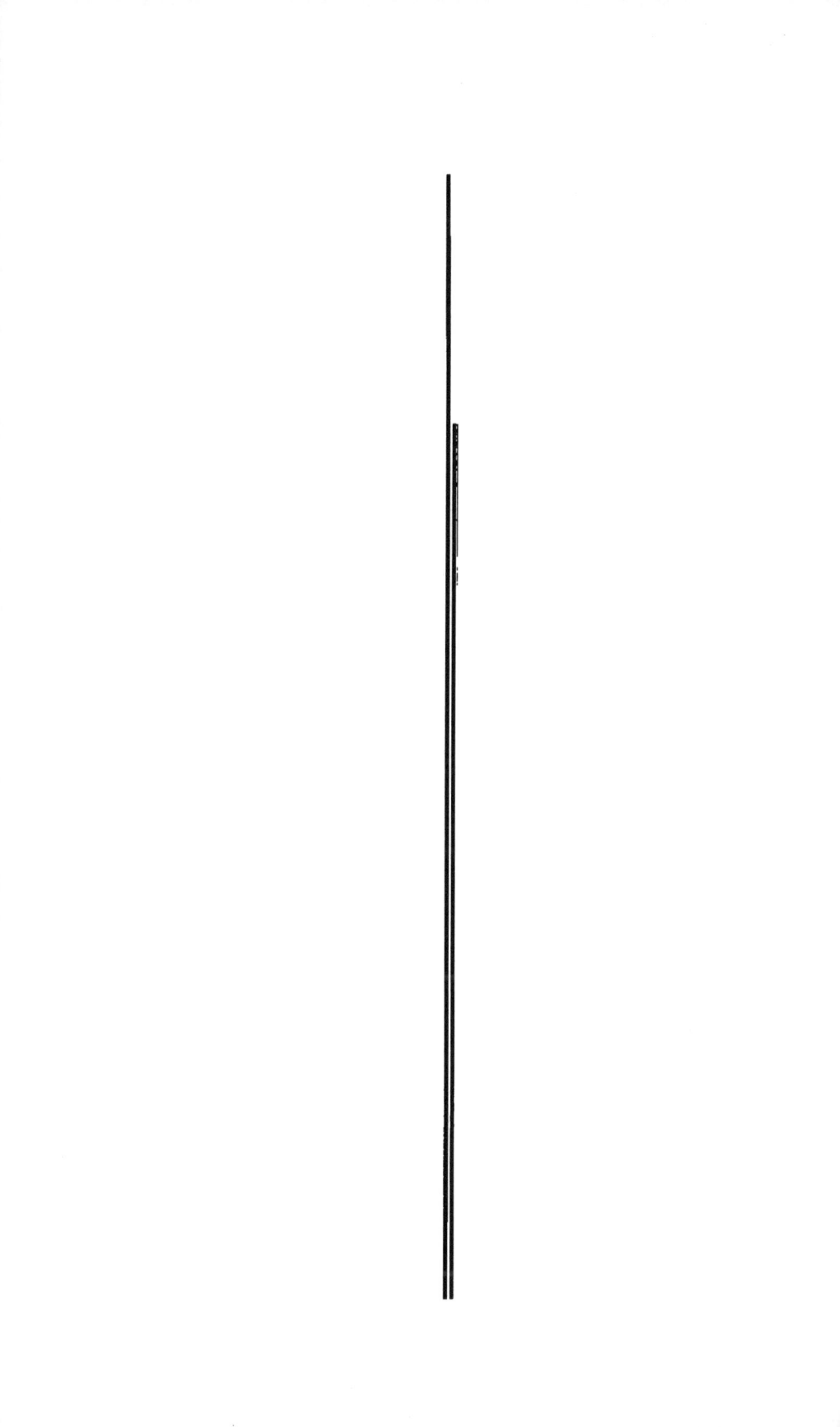

List of Illustrations

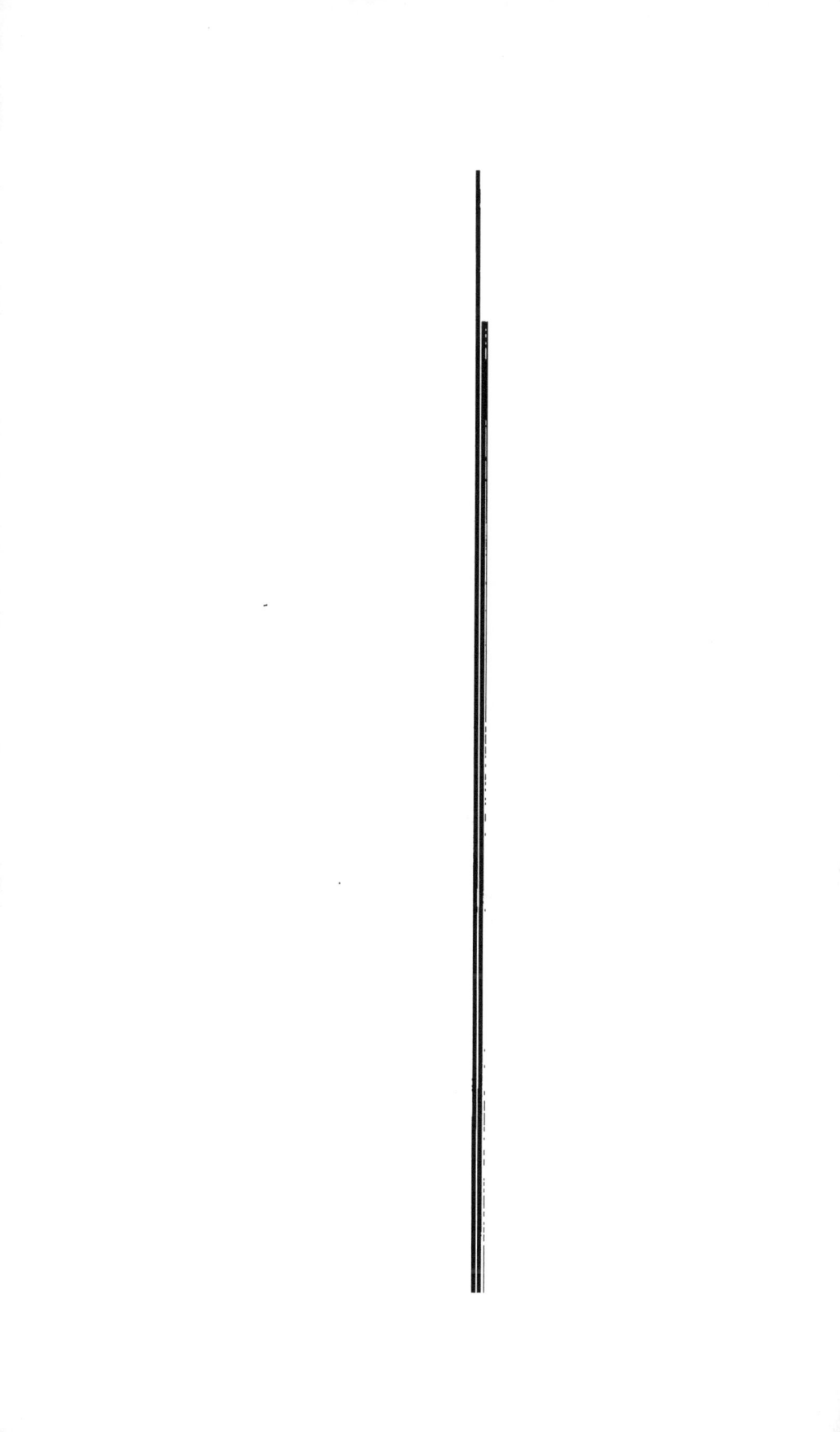

CONTENTS

ii CONTENTS

Part III—Spring

Page

Part IV—Summer

PREFACE

Through the medium of the story, the deepest truths of science can be brought to the child in such a way that his mind will readily grasp the meaning.

Many of these stories were originated for use in my schools and kindergartens; others, including all of the poems, for use later on, in my home, for instruction and entertainment of my own children.

Friends have requested me to publish them, and I have done so, in hopes that they would be instrumental in drawing many children nearer to Nature, and from Nature to Nature's God.

Little folks are eager to hear stories, and it seems wiser to present those calculated to interest them in the world around them; for it is through the systematic study of Nature that their minds are to be developed.

The value of rhymes in child literature can not be overestimated.

If they are too young to read, the mother should repeat them to her children and when they are old enough, they should read the verses for themselves. These poems should interest them in the living things around them, and be the means of helping to find their activities in Nature.

Verses for children should be of simple construction, and language adapted to their understanding; thus they are awakened to the beauties of Nature.

This little volume is intended as a help to teachers and mothers.

The busy mother is often at a loss to find something at hand for the entertainment and instruction of her children.

She wishes to give them Nature Stories and talks for the different seasons of the year; but may be too busy to plan the undertaking of systematic, seasonable lessons.

The teacher in the schoolroom can not have too many helps for her important work with children.

To teachers of the smaller cities and of rural schools (who do not have access to libraries), such a work must fill a long felt need.

The busy teachers of larger cities require helps on Nature Study just as much; for in their vocations, there is but little time for outlining such lessons, and constantly visiting the libraries for something new.

This volume divides into four parts, beginning with *Autumn,* the time of the child starting to school.

This is followed by the *Winter, Spring* and *Summer* departments of stories and verses, coming in the order of the year's school work.

As will be seen by the perusal of the book, it contains Nature Study adaptable to the kindergarten and first four grades.

It is also recommended as supplementary reading for the child at home or at school.

Great stress is laid upon the humane treatment of animals; and the child is taught, through these lessons, not only how to *live* and *see* and *learn,* but of his own true relationship to all life in general.

In many states, teachers are now required to give pupils such instruction, and helpful suggestions may be found here.

March 15, 1912. K. B. J.

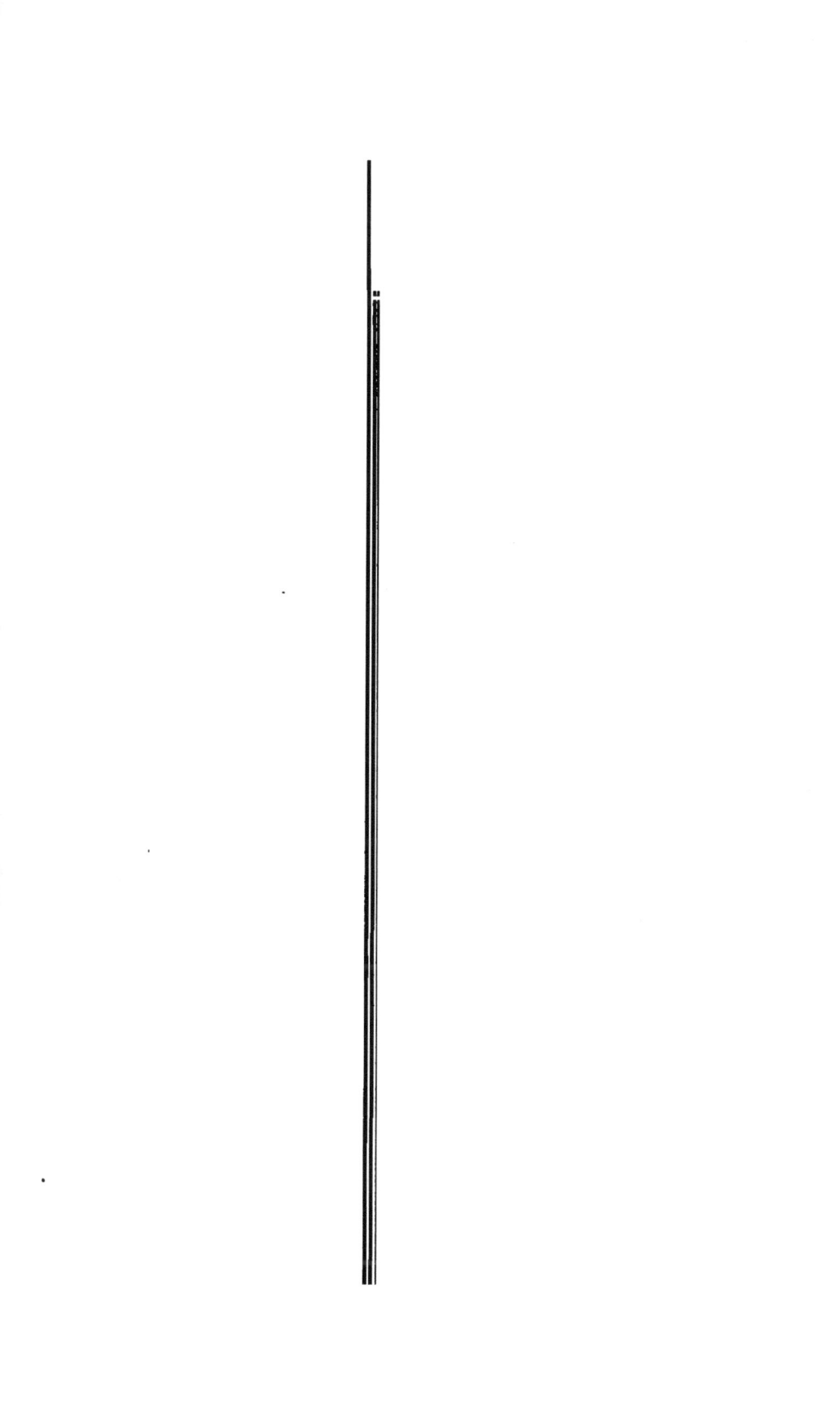

PART ONE

———

AUTUMN

The Leaf Dresses

It was a bright September day, and the wind had been blowing dust in people's eyes and carrying off the children's hats.

The wind hardly ever blows that way unless it has a message to deliver, and the more important the message, the harder it blows.

This particular day, it came from the cold northland to deliver an Autumn secret to the large trees.

The trees had been very proud of their green dresses during the Summer, not only for their beauty, but for the great amount of work they can do. They take the poison out of the air, and make it ready for the people to breathe. They afford a restful color to the eyes, curtain off the birds' nests, and shade the streets and lawns, so people can enjoy a cool walk, or sit and read under their branches. But the wind had brought a message to the trees, a message, saying that the days were much

shorter, cold weather was coming, and all
the trees would soon go to sleep.

The leaves were all to be invited to a
great party, and must begin to put on their
prettiest dresses, so as to be ready.

The trees whispered to the boughs, and
the boughs sent the news down the twigs,
who told their little leaf children all about
it. The leaves were delighted, for they
wanted to frolic with each other, over the
fields. The Maple tree decided to dress her
leaf children in red, and the Cotton-wood,
who was fond of yellow, had hers wear her
favorite color.

Some of the Oaks put on brown and red,
and the next time the wind blew that way,
he took many of the little leaves with him
for a dance. A few Maple leaves decided
they had rather stay on the tree and not
change their gowns, so they clung tightly,
until all the brother and sister leaves had
gone off, and they were left alone.

One of them thought of the flowers who
had grown just beneath her tree, sending
up fragrance and beauty, making everything glad; so she asked the remaining

leaves if they would not go with her, to help cover them.

Some of them decided to go, and the next time the wind came that way, nodded and beckoned to him to take them off.

They covered the violet, while many of their little companions who were left, made the children glad with their rich, red colors.

A dear little girl was looking for leaves and she found a great many, which she took to the kindergarten. They were placed upon a chart so the children could enjoy them in the Winter time.

Autumn Leaves

Old Mother Nature dyed her leaves
  In purple, red and brown,
And cried to children as they passed,
  "How do you like my gown?"

But 'ere the proud old tree could long,
  In this rich dress be clad,
The cold North Wind came sweeping by,
  And what he did was sad!

For, bending bough and twig with might,
  He swept those leaves away;
And soon in heaps upon the ground,
  In colors bright, they lay.

But not in vain! Their mission now
  Had only just begun.
They hid the shivering flowers
  Who missed the Summer's sun.

And children passing home from school,
  Would run around in glee;
And gather lovely Autumn leaves,
  As pleased as they could be.

And there upon the ground some lay,
  'Til rains and Winter's snow
Had changed them into rich leaf mould,
  To make our gardens grow.

Not only those from lofty heights
  Can make the lone hearts glad.
Though small and humble, like the leaves,
  We'll help the poor and sad.

Getting Ready for Winter

"What are you doing?" asked Teddie, as he came home from school one afternoon in September, and saw Uncle George at work in the yard. "Getting ready for Winter," answered Uncle. "Do all people have to get ready for the cold weather?" enquired his little nephew. "Yes," said Uncle George, "and all the animals, birds, and everything else as well. Sit down on that log and I will tell you about it." Teddie sat down, glad of a rest, for he had been running and was quite out of breath. He always ran home, because he was in such a hurry to get back to his dogs, chickens and rabbits, of which he was very fond; and they were fond of him, too, for he took such loving care of them, and always seemed to know what they needed each day to make them happy and keep them well. After Uncle had piled up a few more sticks of wood, he told the following story:

"In the Summer time the sun's rays fall directly upon the earth, and we have warm weather; but in Winter the sun shines more obliquely upon the earth, and we have cold weather, very cold sometimes.

"The people must be kept warm all Winter, and men must work in the dark mines, to get the coal for us to burn.

"The trees which have been growing during the hot weather, make good fuel, but must first be cut down, sawed into pieces of stove length, and seasoned well. I have been getting some of the large, long pieces, the right length for our stove; and after they are well seasoned, we will store them in the cellar, out of the wet.

"We must have kindling wood and coal in the cellar, and many kinds of vegetables, barrels of apples, cans of fruit and preserves, jell, pickles, and many things which must be gathered and prepared during the Summer, and early Fall. The farmer is also very busy with the harvest, and must store away hay and grains of all kinds in the barns and granaries.

"The squirrels know how to prepare for Winter, too, and put away piles of nuts in their hollow trees.

"The birds get ready by going to the warm Southland, where their food can be easily obtained, and not buried by deep snows.

"The caterpillars get ready by spinning their cocoons and taking their long Winter's sleep, ready to come out beautiful butterflies in the Spring.

"The bees get ready by storing honey in their hives. When eating our honey, we must think of the bees, who stored it away so diligently during the Summer time, while the lovely flowers were in bloom.

"Do you know that the carpenter is busy too? All the people are sending for him to come and put up their storm-doors and windows, to repair sheds and barns, and to hurry up the new houses being built.

"If you look around, you will notice that every one is getting ready for the Winter season.

"Grandma is knitting mittens and stockings for the children, and Mother is making new warm dresses and little coats.

"That is all I have time to tell you now, but some other day I will tell you about a great many kinds of birds; those who re-

main with us all winter, and those who do
not."

"That was a fine story," said Teddy, as
he thanked Uncle George and ran away to
play with the boys.

The Carpenter

A Morning Talk for the Kindergarten

At this time of the year, when people are
busy getting ready for Winter, the carpenter must be sent for, to take off our
window screens and put on the storm windows and doors, so our homes will be comfortable during the cold weather.

All the unfinished homes are being hur-
ried, for the people are anxious to get into
them soon.

"Can you tell me of some of the things
the carpenter makes for us?"   "Sidewalks,
pigeon-houses, barns and sheds."   "Yes,
and many other things.   Now, let us see
some of the tools he uses.   What is this
one?"   "A hammer."   "For what does he
use it?"   "To drive the nails in with."
"And this?"   "A plane, to make the rough

boards smooth." "How does he make the long boards shorter?" "With a saw."

To-morrow you may each bring something that is used by the carpenter, and we will make a carpenter's chart. Also bring pictures of him, working at his trade.

Seeds

In the Autumn, there are many little treasure houses to be stored away.

Can you guess what they are? Yes, seeds of all kinds.

They are very precious, as the baby plants lie sleeping within them.

The gardener cares for his seeds, and keeps them in a dry place until Spring.

Every Fall he must attend to this, that he may be ready in the Spring to make his garden.

But there are many seeds that are not gathered at all. What becomes of them?

Some are sent out by the wind and scattered everywhere. The dandelion and milkweed, with their feathery seeds, easily blown about, are springing up where we do not want them.

Here are some seeds of the maple and box elder trees. We see they have a wing which is thin and light, and the wind easily blows them away. Some little boys call them kites.

The sheep, with its coat of wool, also scatters the seeds. As he rubs against the fences and trees, they fall off, to spring up far from the places where they were raised.

Little birds take seeds in their bills for food, and fly away, often dropping them. So we find they, too, scatter the seeds.

We are going to make paper boxes this morning to hold the seeds you have brought. We will label each kind and stow them away in our cupboard until Spring, when we will have a flower bed made in our school yard, and every child will plant a few of his seeds. Each day we will go out and care for them, and watch them as they creep to the light.

I once heard a story of a little seed who lay asleep in the earth, waiting for the warm Spring sun and rain to waken it.

He kept thinking: "I wonder what I will be?" "I do not want to be a lily, for they are too white; nor a rose, for they have thorns; nor a violet, for they are too small.

"I am sure I will be the finest plant in the world, and have the most beautiful flowers of all."

He awoke, at last, to find himself a weed.

Little children are not like the plants. They can become what they want to be.

If I want to raise morning glories, I must plant morning glory seed.

If I want to raise radishes, I must plant radish seed.

If a child wants to grow up good and lovable, he must sow good seeds (have good thoughts). If he is unselfish, agreeable and loving, he will grow that way.

If he delights in doing wicked things, and in hurting others, he will become like the thorny plants, who hurt all who come in contact with them.

Wouldn't it be much better to be like the beautiful blossoms that give joy to all?

What kind of a little seed are you going to be?

Have you ever heard the song:

"Then, scatter seeds of kindness
For our reaping by and by"?

Ask your mothers to sing it to you when you go home.

We will now make pretty borders and rosettes from some of these maple seeds.

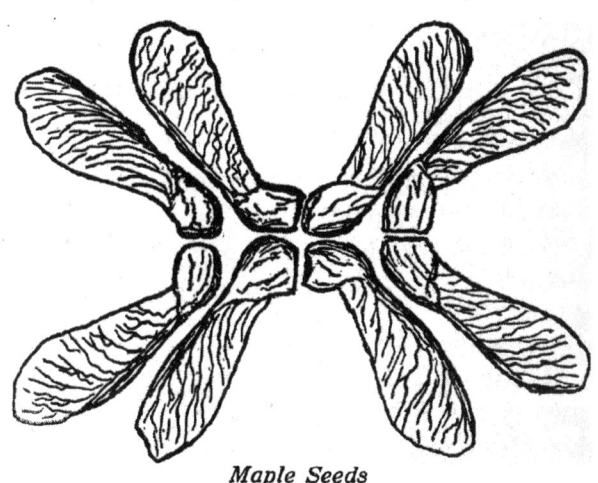

Maple Seeds

The Walnut Tree

Oh, large and noble walnut tree,
  With nuts so round and brown,
When will you leave the branches high
  And come a tumbling down?

I watched you patiently for days,
  While sitting in your shade;
And dreamed of winter hours to come,
  And children happy made,

By walnuts, large and sweet and ripe,
  Cracked by Grandfather dear.
The walnuts which are hanging there
  Will children's hearts soon cheer.

A Thanksgiving Talk

The celebration of Thanksgiving is an old custom, as old as the human race.

The Bible tells us of the "Feast of the Passover," which lasted seven days; six days of feasting, and on the seventh, a day of praises to the Lord. This feast commenced when the corn was being cut.

Nations which had been blessed were to
lend to those which had not been pros-
pered, and those who had abundance were
commanded to give of it to the poor.

We read of a great Thanksgiving celebration in Holland as early as 1575, which
was observed on account of their deliver-
ance from war and other troubles.

It was not like our celebration of
Thanksgiving, for they had carousing and
feasting, entirely leaving out the religious
exercises.

Many hundred years ago, they had
Thanksgiving day in Germany. They
called it the "Grand Feast Day," and cele-
brated it right after the harvest.

When we want to have a celebration, we
have a parade, and men dress in uniform,
and wear caps with big feathers, and carry
guns. So, on their feast day they had a
parade, and men wore gay clothes. Some,
seated on a load of hay, rode through the
streets. The horses wore wreathes of
flowers around their necks. When they
came to the place where they were to have
the feast, they had a dance around the load
of hay. They roasted meat, and had a

great feast, but they didn't have a turkey.
Instead they had peacock. The turkey belonged to America, which had not been
discovered then.

Finally, Columbus came over here from
Spain. After a long voyage across the
ocean, he discovered this land. Once, during the voyage, he turned the wrong way,
but presently he saw some little land birds
flying to the Southwest. He thought he
would follow them. As a result, he landed
in five days at an island called "San Salva-
dor." He and his men were so glad "that
they knelt on the ground and gave thanks
to God." This might be considered the
first Thanksgiving day in America.

A short time after Columbus discovered
America, some other men in Spain thought
they would see what the new land was like.
So they crossed the ocean and went farther
into our country than Columbus did, and
there they saw some Indians who were
having a great feast. The Indians asked
them to eat with them. They did so, and
when they tasted some of the meat called
"turkey," they found it was very different
from anything they had ever eaten. When

they returned home, they took some with
them. Now it is used all over the world.

When we are celebrating our Thanksgiving, the whole United States are ob-
serving it also, for it is a day of National
observance. The people go to church to
thank God for his kindness and the bounti-
ful harvests. In our kindergarten we learn
to sing, "Father, in Heaven, we thank
Thee."

What Shall We Do Thanksgiving

One lovely November morning, Miss
Nellie, who was a kindergartner, had all of
her little pupils march to the circle with
their chairs, and in her morning talk, they
learned much of their relationship to God
and man, for she explained the custom of
keeping Thanksgiving day sacred. I happened to be a visitor, and this is what I
heard her say: "Children, we all have
something to be thankful for, have we
not?" "Yes," they replied, "many things."
"Marion may name some of the things she
is thankful for." Marion said, "dogs, good
food, and clothes, papa, mama, and my little brother." "Yes, we should all thank

God for every good thing he gives us."
All of the little ones told of many things
for which they were thankful. They sang
the following song:
"Father, we thank Thee for the night,
And for the pleasant morning light;
For rest, and food, and loving care,
And all that makes the world so fair."

They decided upon a lovely idea, which
was to have a barrel in their kindergarten,
and let each child bring something to put
in it as a gift for the poor. Many could
bring aprons, dresses, waists, and other
things which they had outgrown.

So the barrel was filled, and many a poor
child made glad, by apples, oranges, and
good things, which perhaps they had seldom tasted.

Many received the first clothes they had
ever had that were suitable for church
wear. Thus we may all do good, not only
on Thanksgiving day, but *every day.*

Happy Autumn Days

The days are not melancholy
  In the Autumn of the year,
For this time of happy harvest
  Brings to each of us good cheer.

There is much to be provided
  For the good of hungry men,
And what's grown and become ripened,
  Can be gathered in right then.

We'll not grumble at the seasons,
  For each one of us must see
How with wisdom the Creator,
  Thinks of you, and thinks of me.

Then, let every one be thankful
  On the glad Thanksgiving Day,
For the goodness of the Giver,
  We *with gratitude* can pay.

Kindergarten Baking Exercise

We jolly little bakers
  With white caps on our heads,
Can make you anything you wish,
  From cookies down to bread.

We will roll our dough with skill,
  And shape you what you will.
Whether cookies, tarts, or pies,
  You will find them very nice.

Baking Song

With our sleeves rolled up,
And our aprons on,
  We are little bakers gay.
See our pies and cakes,
'And our nice light bread!
  Oh, what a fine array!

Busy farmers plant,
Busy millers grind,
  That we good white flour may use.
We are ready now,
And will make for you,
  Cookies, bread, or what you choose.

In our oven hot
We will put the dough,
  Taking care it shall not burn.
Soon we'll pass some cakes,
If you will but wait,
  And you'll see what we have learned.

Apple Pie

Mix a little flour,
  Water, salt and lard;
Roll it out, my little one,
  Roll it now, quite hard!

When the dough, so round,
  Has covered up the tin,
Fill it with sliced apples
  And throw seasoning in.

Then we make a cover,
  Of some more dough.
Soon it's baked and ready.
  Children laugh and crow!

The Loaf of Bread

"Daisy, come, go to the store for a loaf of bread!" called mama.

The little girl came skipping in for the money, and was soon in the bakery.

Everything smelled fresh and good, and she bought a nice loaf of bread, which she took home.

After eating a hearty supper, she played quite a while, then went into the house to read.

Presently, she was listening to the story of a loaf of bread, for it seemed to speak thus:

"I was once a tiny wheat grain, who, with a bushel of others like myself, were purchased by Farmer Brown. He then planted us, and though I was glad to get out of the bag, I did not like the dark earth.

"Soon the Spring rains fell, and I began to hope, for I somehow felt I might be able to leave my dark prison.

"My hopes ran so high, I began to swell, and actually sent up a tiny green shoot to greet the sun.   It seemed as if the warm air and sunshine were drawing me up, while my roots kept growing deeper, and drank in the food I required to make me grow into a beautiful plant.

"I looked around.   Up were springing all of my little companions, who had been in the bag with me; and we nodded to each other.

"Time went on, and Farmer Brown was proud of his 'wheat field,' as he called it, and said 'he was to have a fine crop.'

"After a while we were a field of yellow, ripened grain, and were gathered, threshed, and sold to the miller.

"At his mill we were made into flour, and put into nice clean white sacks with bright letters painted on them.

"We were then sold to a store, where we were soon disposed of to the people.

"A nice lady bought the bag into which I was put, and the boy delivered me to her home.

"I was emptied into a flour bin in her kitchen cabinet, and the next time she baked, I was made into a loaf of nice white bread.

"They had the loaf, in which I now staid, for supper."

"Then how can you tell this story?" you ask, "if they had you for supper?"

"I will tell you. I happened to be in the crust, and the little girl who took my slice, did not like crusts; so she hid me under the edge of her plate.

"This was rather naughty of her, for her mama did not want her to be wasteful, and often told her of the many poor children who need food to eat.

"There is no telling what will happen to me next, for here the maid comes to brush away the crumbs. So, good-by."

Daisy sat up and rubbed her eyes, saying, "I will *never* throw away any more crusts."

Little Lillian Edna Blue

Little Lillian Edna Blue
Ha'd to work the whole day through.
She always did whatever told,
'Though she was but ten years old.

"Now," said Lillian Edna Blue,
"Please don't give me much to do.
I get tired as well as the rest,
And I always do my best."

If an idle moment she had,
'Twas considered very bad,
For so much precious time to waste,
And of childish pleasures taste.

Lillian had a dream one night,
Of a land both fair and bright,
Where little children, dear and sweet,
Have nothing to do—*but eat.*

Where nice plum-puddings grow on trees,
And good honey from the bees;
Some cookies, candies, pies and fruit,
Oh, how could they help but suit!

She thought the children gathered round,
Eating goodies they had found;
For they came tumbling off the tree,
Piling in their laps, you see!

But as they all the feast begin,
A great bear had to step in.
They were so frightened that they fled,
Leaving him the buttered bread.

For, having chased them all away,
Mr. Bear was now quite gay;
And soon the feast, he in his might,
Could pronounce "quite out of sight."

Then next he looked around to see
If he had not better flee.
But this he found he could not do,
And I tell you, he was *blue;*

For, scamp'ring through the woods once
        more,
Came the children, just a score,
To beat him with an ugly stick!
I am sure it made him sick.

When little Lillian awoke,
She found 'twas a "dreamed up" joke;
For she alone lay on the mound.
Not a Bear was there around,

Except her own dear Teddy Bear
Who was sleeping on a chair.
"How innocent you look!" said she,
'Twas not you who frightened me."

She rubbed her eyes, and went to work,
Saying, "I will never shirk.
'Tis nicer to help mama bake
Than to give the trees a shake,

And scamper off to pick up pies,
Cookies too, and all things nice.
I'll make the things I ought to make,
And not be afraid to bake."

The Squirrel Family

In a large, hollow tree in the forest, lived two squirrels, with their family of little ones, consisting of Budge and Betty.

There was no tree as nice as the one they lived in, and no family any happier than theirs.

Budge and Betty chased each other up and down among the branches, played hide and seek in the leaves, and were as happy and free from care as any two little squirrels you ever saw.

They were acquainted with the birds who sang to them from the trees, and picked up the kernels of nuts which they dropped.

They made friends with the rabbits and gophers, who were their neighbors; but the delight of their hearts was to play with their cousin squirrels, who lived near by.

All summer they ran and played and grew very strong.

When the cooler days came, they were surprised to see the leaves which had been

such a beautiful green, change to colors of
red, yellow and gold. What did it all
mean? Budge looked at Betty to see if her
fur was not turning red; and Betty looked
at Budge to see if he was not changing to
another color. It seemed as if the entire
world was changing.

The chestnut burrs were being opened
by the frost, and all the nuts were falling.

Mr. and Mrs. Squirrel were busy every
day, gathering nuts for the Winter, for
they had lived long enough to know that it
would soon be cold, with deep snow, and
no chance to find any food, except what had
been stored away in their pantry.

To provide for four little hungry
mouths was no small task. They wasted
no time, but cold weather came much sooner than they had expected; and Mr. Squirrel became worried for fear they would
not have sufficient food laid away before
snow came. So he called Budge to him and
said: "Now, Budge, you are growing fast,
and are so strong and frisky for play, that
I think you should use some of your
strength in helping us lay up food for
Winter. You are much stronger than

Betty, and I dare say, even she can do a little to help."

Budge, who had never been taught to work, thought it pretty hard to be called upon; but he told Betty, and they set to work, carrying in nuts. Betty worked all day, only stopping now and then to rest; but Budge grew very tired before he had put away enough nuts for one meal for himself. Then he lay down and rested.

The next day was cloudy and cold, and the squirrels all thought it was going to snow before night; so they went to work with a will. Mr. and Mrs. Squirrel said: "If we all work hard, we will, before dark, have enough nuts to last all winter."

They all started in search of nuts, and were so busy they never stopped to speak to each other.

It was some time before they noticed that Budge had disappeared and was no-where around.

The rest worked all the harder then, for there was one less to work, and four to eat.

Budge, who was attracted by some squirrels who were playing near by, ran off to have a frolic with them; and after a game of tag among the leaves, he started home, but was caught in a trap which some boys had set.

Poor Budge! He was so frightened he could hardly breathe; and when the boys said, "Let's take him home and make a pet of him," he thought that must be something terrible, and shook like a leaf.

"Now, I will be made into a pet," he said, "when I might have stayed with mother and helped her."

The boys soon reached their home, which was a small frame cottage, with no trees around it. Budge thought he would die if he had to live there. It was so unhomelike!

It grew dark, and the boys, having no cage, fixed a box for their pet, thinking it would do until they had time to get a nice cage.

Budge lay down on some straw in the corner and pretended to sleep, but was all the time thinking of his cozy nest in his tree home in the forest.

In the meantime, his father, mother and

sister Betty were wondering where he could be, and wishing for his safe return.

All night he slept in the box, poor, little frightened Budge, too scared to know that he might easily have escaped from such a dilapidated abode as the one the boys had prepared. When they awoke in the morning, the first thing they did was to visit the box; and finding it as they left it, and the squirrel seemingly contented, they said: "We will use the box a few days until father comes home and gets a new cage for us."

Their sister insisted that they must not keep the pet, as she wanted the fur for a collar.

Budge began to wish he was away from there, and made up his mind to try to get out. So when all the family had retired, he set to work nibbling a small hole in one corner of the box, being careful to cover it over with straw when any one was around. All that night he worked, and all the next day, as the family had gone away for a visit.

By the middle of the night he could push

his way out, and away he ran to meet his family in the woods.

It was dark, cold, and snow was falling. He thought of the nuts, and had visions of long, cold days, with nothing to eat, because he had not minded his parents.

Perhaps it would have been better for him to have stayed with the boys and let them have him for the collar.

He was sure his sister Betty would be ashamed of him now, and would never want to see him again.

Once or twice he turned back, but at last made up his mind to stand the rebuke he deserved, like a brave little squirrel.

He arrived at the tree at last and entered the room where his mother, father, and sister were all having breakfast.

They were greatly surprised to see Budge, and anxious to hear his story.

All were glad to have him back once more, and invited in the neighbor squirrels and cousins to have a great feast in his honor.

Budge is very happy now, and not a bit lazy, for he thinks it better to spend part of the time working.

Every Autumn finds him the most industrious squirrel in the forest; and with nuts to spare for a large squirrel banquet.

The First Gift Balls

RED AND ORANGE

My ball is a little apple,
  So red and round and ripe,
And mine is a juicy orange,
  So pretty and so bright.

YELLOW AND GREEN

Mine is a yellow butterfly,
  Who flits among the flowers;
And this is little Poll Parrot,
  The talking bird of ours.

BLUE AND VIOLET

Mine is a bit of bright blue sky,
  From out the heavens blue,
And this is little violet,
  All wet with morning dew.

The Little Balls As Fruits

Six little balls
   Hanging on the trees!
Six little balls,
   Swinging in the breeze!

Red, lovely ball,
   Hanging on the tree,
Just drop this way,
   Apple ripe, for me.

Round, orange ball
   Called to little Pearl,
"I'm an orange!
   Eat me, little girl!"

Nice yellow ball,
   Swinging in the shade,
You're a lemon,
   Good for lemonade.

Now our green ball,
   Is an apple sour.
Bad boy took him!
   In pain for an hour!

See the blue balls!
  We must all have some,
For they will be
  Our delicious plums.

Rich purple ball,
  Beautiful to see,
Fall right down here,
  Be a grape for me.

The Six Balls

My little red ball
  Is like clover
That blooms the grassy
  Meadows over.

Mine, an orange ball,
  Like fruit that's ripe,
Or the sunset clouds,
  So fair and bright.

My yellow ball is
  A butterfly,
Who, to the cocoon
  Has said "good-by."

This, like a parrot
  So green, can fly,
But it can not talk
  If it should try.

Here is one that's blue.
  Do look and see
How like May's blue eyes
  It tries to be!

This last ball is like
  The violet,
And in the pansies
  Too, it is met.

The Second Gift

My second gift house
  Is made of hard wood.
The children in it
  Are all very good.

Move the sliding door,
  And then take a peep.
Ah! there they all are,
  So soundly asleep!

We will ask them now
   To come out and play,
Right on our table,
   Said Robbie and May.

They looked in the box
   With wide open eyes,
Sphere, cube and cylinder,
   The children then spy!

Three dear little friends,
   All made of smooth wood,
All very happy,
   And most always good.

The sphere was quite glad
   To come out and roll
Like any other
   Dear little round ball;

But lazy cube said,
   "I prefer to rest
Right in the corner
   Of my little nest."

Then cried cylinder,
   "I can roll and slide.
Brother sphere and I
   Could help if we tried

To push you along,
   Since you cannot run!
So come on and play,
   And enjoy the fun."

So little cube crept
   From out of her box;
And with help she slid
   As still as a fox.

They chased each other
   Until tired of play,
Then, in their snug house
   They were put away.

The house was then closed,
   All firmly and tight;
And the dear children
   Wished them a "good night."

My Cat

I have a little pet at home,
   And when her fur you're stroking,
She sings a song that's very sweet
   And not at all provoking.

She purrs so loudly, I'm afraid
   You might think she was a bird.
No doubt, of the little cushions
   On her four feet, you have heard.

She wears them so little mousie
   Will never hear her coming;
But if he feels her strong, sharp claws,
   He will not think her cunning.

If she could talk, I think she'd say:
   "I'm so glad I'm not like boys,
With heavy shoes upon their feet,
   Filling the house with their noise."

Now can you guess who my pet is?
   Why, it is my cat so good.
I mean to always treat her well
   And will see that she has food.

A Little Rosa Bonheur

A little girl was told
　　Of Rosa Bonheur's fame,
And of how she studied
　　The animals so tame,

Before she tried to paint
　　Their pictures true to life;
And in her industry
　　She soon had pictures rife,

Which sold for great prices
　　All over the nation;
Those wonderful paintings
　　Of her own creation.

So she told her kittie
　　That she believed that she
Would get books about her,
　　And study carefully.

After she had read books
　　On the subject of cats,
She had puss pose for her
　　And made a picture that

I'm sure you'd think lifelike
  For it looked like a *cat*.
Her brother Ted bought it,
  What do you think of that?

PART TWO

WINTER

Howard sat down on the Sled

Jack Frost

It was a November night, and a wee little girl had been tucked snugly in her warm bed by her mother's loving hands; and her lips had felt the sweet kiss, as they bade each other "good night."

The room was comfortable, for a bright fire glowed on the hearth, and the clock, ticking loudly, was all the sound to be heard.

A little later, and all in the house had retired for the night.

The moon shone brightly, and the air was becoming colder out of doors, for North Wind and Jack Frost had decided to go out together for a little fun.

North Wind tugged at a man's hat, and sent it flying away. He then rattled the windows and doors, as if to waken the sleepers.

Jack Frost went to work in a more quiet way, and when the little girl awoke next morning, the first thing she spied was the beautiful window-panes, on which Jack had left his work, as fine as lace. There

were pictures of trees, ferns, leaves, and
mountains.

When she tried to take a drink from her
little cup, she saw that a great joke had
been played on her, for the water had been
turned to ice. "Mama," she cried, "do
come and see the window, and here is the
water all frozen." "Get right back into
bed," said mama, "for it is very cold. Jack
Frost was out last night." "I don't like
him," said the little girl. Then her mama
told her that we would have no sleigh-
rides, coasting, or ice cream if it was not
for Jack Frost. "Then I guess I will like
him after all," she replied.

What the Coal Said

The wind was howling and whistling
without, and driving the snow into great
banks; but within, all was quiet and comfortable.

Before the warm fire in the grate, sat
three little children, who had not noticed
that it was growing late, so intent were
they upon the stories they were telling.
At last one little curly head was seen to

bump against the back of the chair, and the eyelids closed over the blue eyes. The others, not noticing her, went on with their stories, and pretty soon, in came mama to tell them it was time to go to bed.

She gave Bessie, the one who was asleep, a shake to waken her; and Bess rubbed her eyes, and said: "Oh. mama, let me tell you the funny story the Coal was just telling me!"

"All right," said mama, taking her on her lap. This is the story as she repeated it:

"You children have been talking, and never gave me a chance.

"I suppose you think a piece of black coal, put in the fire to burn, has nothing to tell; but I know the most wonderful story about myself—just *wonderful*.

"I am really very old, older than you think. I lived years ago, before there were any people on the earth, no little boys and girls, animals or flowers.

"Then I did not look as I do now. My brother and sister lumps of coal around me were once trees, ferns, or some kind of tropical plants, growing to a great height. The sun shone with intense heat, and our branches and leaves drank in all the sunshine they could.

"After a time, the sun was hidden behind the clouds. The rain fell and the ground became so soft it actually sank— until the trees were carried from view. Then the wind blew, and the fiery sun shone out again, and dried the soft earth.

"Other tropical plants grew up and waved their branches to and fro in the sunshine; and they, too, sank and were hidden from view.

This period was called the 'Age of Carbon.' In the earth, these plants were subjected to great heat and pressure, and formed what was called 'coal.'

"Did you say that you could not believe it? Well, it has been proven to be true, from the fossil remains found in the mines. In clay beds, at the bottoms of mines, pictures of roots were found; and in the clay roofs, were found pictures of leaves, and ferns, which plainly told the story, and showed that some of the trees must have been very tall.

"In the coal itself, impressions of ferns and various plants have been seen. There are two kinds of coal, the anthracite or hard coal, and the bituminous or soft coal.

"The hard coal, in its formation, received greater pressure and heat. It gives out scarcely any flame and does not burn so quickly.

"The soft coal gives a bright flame, as oils and gases are contained in it in large quantities. It · received less heat and pressure than hard coal."

"Now," said the wise piece of coal, "when you look at us, you must think first of sunshine, then of trees, then of coal.

"If you sit by a wood fire on a cold night, do not forget that every stick of wood you are burning has sunbeams packed away in it. The tree to which the stick of wood once belonged, set all of 'his leaves to work to catch sunbeams and store them away in the limbs, to form fuel for our future use. Just think how many of the sun's rays were stowed away in each lump of coal you burn!

"When I lay in the ground, I thought I never would get out of the dark prison and be of use in the world; but at last a great shaft was sunk, until it reached the coal bed where I lay.

"I was very happy when the men, each with a little light on his cap, came down into the dark mine, to work with picks and mine the coal which was to keep the children warm."

"That is all of it," said Bessie, "for you came and shook me, and the coal stopped talking."

"That was a very good story, and a true one," said mama. "We will let her dream again some time, won't we children?"

Mending Day

Mother was doing the mending,
    And putting the garments down
In neat and even little piles
    In the basket large and brown.

Each garment, as she was mending,
    Seemed its own story to tell.
First, came a dress for her darling,
    Her own careless little Nell.

Had she not had the misfortune
  To get caught on an old nail,
I fear you never would have heard
  Of this sad yet truthful tale.

The next, a little blouse of blue,
  For John, so lively and gay,
Who met with many sudden tears,
  When with the children at play.

Button-waists minus the buttons!
  Her addition problem's soon done.
She places them in the basket
  And picks up another one.

So on and on she keeps mending,
  'Til all are as good as new.
In closets and drawers she stores them,
  The good mother kind and true.

Oh, what would we do without her,
  When she does so much for us?
No wonder the children love her,
  And make such a stir and fuss.

She is most devoured by kisses,
  For this household angel true,
Liveth not for herself alone,
  But does the good she can do.

A Snowflake Story

One beautiful Winter day, the large, white snowflakes were falling.

The children were already clapping their hands, crying with delight, for it meant to them, snowmen, snowballs, sleigh rides, coasting, and many other Winter games which can be played in the snow.

Little Howard ran to the shed to drag out his nice new sled, which had been stored there.

This was the first snowstorm of the year, and here was a chance to use it.

The flakes now fell faster and faster, and one very large one of beautiful shape, fell on the bright sled.

Howard sat down on the sled and looked at it carefully and with great interest.

His nature work at school had taught him to examine even the smallest of the beautiful things God has given us.

Howard almost forgot that he intended to go coasting, as the Flake said:

"Well, I must say, this swift traveling makes me dizzy. I am very tried." Howard was so startled, he almost fell off the sled, but he kept quiet for fear of stopping the little frosty voice.

After a short rest the snowflake became more friendly than ever, and continued: "I wonder, little boy, if you have ever taken as long a journey as the one I just took?"

Howard asked the Flake, "if he had been up very high?"

"Well, I should think so," replied the Snowflake. "If you care to listen, I will tell you the story of my life."

Howard gladly listened, for he wanted to know all about the snow he was going to ride over.

"Long ago," said the Flake, "I lived in a large place called the Ocean. There were all sorts of fine fishes, seaweeds, sponges, shells, and many things besides."

"I was called 'Aqua,' for aqua, you know, means water, and that was what I was when I lived there.

"I used to play and splash with my little brother and sister waterdrops, and have

good times.   Being very happy, I was in
no hurry to have the sunbeams take me
up to cloudland, as our Mother Ocean
had said they would, in time.

"But one day, when playing with my
little friends, I felt myself lifted up, and
felt ever so queer.

"I could see, by looking at my brothers
near me, that they were changing to
vapor, and rising quite fast. I knew I
was doing the same, and before long, was
up so high that I dared not look down at
the earth beneath me. We were blown
by the wind, now here, now there, and
finally came close together, forming what
people called 'clouds.'   That was long
ago, when I was quite young. I remained
in the clouds a long time, it seemed to me,
and the wind blew them into all sorts of
beautiful shapes.

"Sometimes we journeyed so high that
I grew very cold. During the night the
clouds had a discussion to decide what to
do with us. The largest cloud, who
seemed to be commander, declared we
must be dropped, as we were getting
quite heavy.

"We almost turned blue at the thought of being dropped, oh, ever so far!"

"Pretty soon, something icy cold struck us, and gave us all a white color, and made us shiver.

"I expected a dreadful fall, but we all came down so quietly and gently that no one knew we were on our way.

"We do not all look alike. Some of us are nearly round, some star-shaped, and other curious forms.

"I don't think I can live much longer, as I feel weak and can scarcely speak!"

Howard, who had been strangely quiet and interested, looked closely and saw the snowflake melting. In place of it, there stood a large, round tear-drop.

His dark eyes grew rounder as he rubbed them, and he didn't even speak to his mother, who came to call him to supper.

Little Snowflakes

Welcome, little snowflakes,
  In your dresses white!
You covered field and vale
  As you fell last night.

Welcome, little fairies;
  For you dress the earth,
Covering up its blackness,
  Bringing children mirth.

Without you, no snowman,
  And the sleigh-rides, too.
Darling little snowflakes!
  How we all love you.

Story of the Christ Child

Long ago, in a far off country, some Shepherds were in the fields, caring for their flocks of sheep by night.

As they sat talking and watching, suddenly they saw a bright light, and in the glory of the light, an Angel. They were quite frightened, but the Angel said: "Fear not, I have good news for you, and for all the people in the world. There was born this day, in Bethlehem, a babe who is to be a Saviour. His name is Christ the Lord. You will find him lying in a manger."

Then the Angel told the Shepherds which way to go to find the wonderful child, and they heard singing, which was beautiful, for there were many Angels who had come to bring the good tidings. They sang: "Glory to God in the highest, and on earth, *peace,* good-will toward men."

Then the Angels went back to Heaven, and the Shepherds said, "Let us go to Bethlehem and see if this is true."

So they set out in haste, until they came to the place where the babe was, with his mother. They did not find him in a fine house, for the houses were all full; but he was in a place called a "stable," and his cradle was a manger.

Then the Shepherds repeated what the Angels had told and sung, and the people were filled with wonder. The mother of the babe thought about what it all meant.

The Shepherds went back to their work, singing and praising God as they went.

There were other people who came to find Jesus.

On the night the Angels sang their song, some *wise men,* in a far off country, saw the bright light in the sky. It seemed like a beautiful star, and as they looked, it moved on and on, until it seemed to be showing them the *way* to go.

So the Wise Men followed the star, until by-and-by, it stood quite still. Then they found they had come to the place where the baby Jesus was.

When they saw the little Jesus, they laid gifts of gold and other good things at his feet, and bowed their heads in prayer.

This was the first Christmas, and these were the first Christmas gifts anybody ever gave.

Christmas Welcome

Welcome, friends, and "Merry Christ-
    mas,"
  To each one we gladly call!
Welcome to our happy schoolroom—
  Welcome, welcome, to you all!

We are just right glad you found us,
  And we'll speak for you, and sing.
We will tell you of the Christ-Child
  Who was sent to be our King.

Welcomes rang through every Nation
   Christmas day, when He was born.
Angels' voices sweetly echoed
   On that happy Christmas morn.

For the blessed Christ-Child Baby,
   In the manger far away,
Came to make the whole world happy
   On that joyful Christmas Day.

Santa Claus' Helper

When from the sky dear Mother Nature
   Is throwing snowflakes down,
Up in his home, among his playthings,
   Old Santa sits him down;

And at his list he keenly glances
   To see which girls and boys
Have been real good since last he saw
     them,
   And which deserve most toys.

His list is long, but all the numbers
   Of houses soon he knows!
He packs the baskets full of good things,
   Then in his sleigh he goes.

He cracks his whip, and on he hurries
  To please each darling child;
And cares not he for wintry weather
  Nor craves for summer mild.

But what is this? A tiny newsboy,
  (No home or shelter he)!
Has sunk exhausted on the pavement,
  As cold as he can be!

Old Santa, then, in just a twinkling,
  The little one espied,
And in his sleigh he quickly took him,
  And gave the lad a ride.

All wrapped in furs, he soon in comfort,
  Could sing in childish glee,
For, although he had seen eight summers,
  For'him, no Christmas Tree,

Or Santa Claus with lovely presents,
  And goodies from Saint Nick!
I'm sure that Santa quickly guessed it.
  He piled the presents thick!

And such a happy little newsboy,
  For Santa took him home
To be his helper, up in toyland.
  No more he had to roam.

The New Year Talk

The New Year has come, and how glad we are.

He was ushered in with ringing of bells and blowing of whistles, and every one is glad to have a New Year in which to grow and learn.

We can look back over our past mistakes and improve upon them. We will resolve to grow three ways—larger, better and wiser.

This is the day for everyone to turn over a new leaf and begin on a clean white page to make a new and better record.

We must decide what kind of a record we really want, and try to do our best.

Then let us all be glad and wish every one we see a "Happy New Year."

The Little New Year

Who comes sliding o'er the ice?
'Tis the little New Year nice.
He has come a while to stay
While the children with him play.

They'll enjoy his ice and snow,
And will hate to see him go.
Now, hurrah for all the fun
As we frolic, every one!

Abraham Lincoln

Abraham Lincoln, like Washington,
was born in February.

We always think of these two great
men this month, and love to celebrate
their birthdays because they were brave,
truthful and honest.

Abraham Lincoln was born in 1809
and lived until 1865.

Although he had but meager oppor-
tunities for education, yet he studied by
himself and was very fond of books.

He wanted to study all of the time, and take his books with him when he went to work, that he might read when resting.

His stepmother was very kind, and although his father opposed so much reading and studying both day and night, she encouraged him, and he was allowed to read whenever he liked and until he was ready to stop.

He had but few books, but they were the best to be obtained at that time. The Bible, Pilgrim's Progress, Robinson Crusoe and Aesop's Fables he read until late at night, by the poor light of the fire. Very early in the morning he arose to study again.

It was said that he borrowed every book in that country for fifty miles around.

A History of the United States and Weems's Life of Washington greatly pleased him, and influenced his political career later.

He not only read what others had written, but he was always writing, trying to express their meaning in his own manner.

He would scribble on anything, a piece of board, a shovel, or bit of cardboard, or anything he could find, only so he could jot down his ideas.

When ploughing, he would take a book from his pocket occasionally, glance at some favorite topic, then close it and go on.

His work was a pleasure to him, for his mind was active, and seemed to lift him above the common clod with which he was dealing unto higher ideals.

While the plough was making the furrow in the ground, the thoughts of the author he was studying, ploughed their way into his mind.

At night he often lay awake trying to express the same ideas in his own language. This self-education made him a clear thinker and speaker; also a great writer, and he was considered a very entertaining bright man of the time in which he lived.

He had less than one entire year of schooling in his life, so we see he was a self-made man.

He was a great lover of Nature and appreciated the flowers and trees. The birds and animals found in him a friend who cared for and petted them.

He was once on his way to go to an important meeting when he saw, in the road, a little bird's nest with young birds in it. Although in a great hurry, he left his horse and climbed the tree to replace the little nest.

At an early age he did a man's work and was unusually strong.

When they settled in Illinois, he helped cut down the trees and make the logs from which their little log house was to be built.

He was not afraid to work, and any boy who is not afraid of hard work and study, is going to amount to something.

We all know how he became President of the United States.

When you are older you will study the life of this great man, who made such a record for honesty that he was called: "Honest Old Abe."

Our Flag

Of the flags that I have seen
  Of many kinds and every hue,
There is none that's half so grand
  As our own dear red, white and blue.

Then wave our flag of freedom!
  Our banner for truth and the right.
As it floats o'er land and sea
  We are proud of our colors bright.

Soft breezes float it on high,
  While heaven smiles down from above,
As our bright banner proclaims
  We're a Nation of peace and love.

Let us proudly wave our flag!
  For it tells of battles won,
And of our fight for freedom
  For each brave American.

Hurrah for our country's flag!
  Hurrah for the *red, white* and *blue!*
Red is for love, the blue is truth,
  White in purity waves for you.

George Washington

George Washington was born the 22d day of February, 1732, and that is why I must tell you about him today.

His birthday will soon be here. If he were still living, he would be 180 years old the 22d day of this month.

He was a good little boy, who loved his mother very much; and although he lived so many years ago, when there were no kindergartens in our country, nor very good schools, yet he tried hard to learn a great deal.

His mother had taught him to improve his time; and he minded her, because he loved her and knew she was always right.

Was it any wonder he grew up to be a brave and good boy; and became a good man?

He was very tall and strong when he became a young man, and could lift (all alone), a heavy tent which it took several men usually to lift, and throw it into a wagon.

He was one of our best Generals, and became the first President of the United States.

George Washington was always right on time, when a boy—never late to school or church; and when he grew up, he was always punctual about everything he did.

If he engaged to meet Congress at noon, he was always at the door at twelve. He dined at four o'clock; and if others were invited in, dinner went on just the same, at the appointed hour. If any came late, he said, "Gentlemen, we are punctual here."

He tried to be polite, and liked to have everybody else be.

It was he who wrote the "Rules for Behavior," which all children should learn and practice.

As you all know how truthful he was, I will not tell you the story of his hatchet and the cherry tree.

Brave Washington

Oh, Washington, we honor thee;
   For among the brave you stood,
Caring for your country nobly,
   Living only for the good.

When a boy, you always minded
   Your dear mother kind and true;
So you grew up strong and noble,
   As the good boys always do.

And your father was so happy,
   For the truth you always spoke,
Not a lie your lips escaping,
   No—not even for a joke.

So you kept the laws of country,
   Of the home, and of the schools,
And you gave to little children
   All those fine behavior rules.

We will study them, endeavoring
   To become polite, like thee;
But there's one thing we'll remember!
   How you cut the cherry tree!

What Became of the Teapot

Two little girls, Mabel and Alice, lived in the country with their parents, in a splendid farm house.

They used to romp through the house in winter, and play hide and seek, there were so many rooms and closets that made good hiding places.

In a large cupboard, mama used to keep a great many of her choice pieces of china, and some old-fashioned relics, which she considered too valuable to use, as they could not be replaced if broken.

One day the children had been playing and having great fun, when their mother who sat in a room up stairs, heard a noise.

She waited to see if the girls would come up and tell her what they had done. Soon Alice came running up, crying, "Oh, mama, I have broken your teapot—the one you thought so much of!"

"I didn't mean to, but you see, I went into the cupboard to hide, and you told us never to go in there, but I didn't mind you."

"You must remember," said mama, "that I also told you that little girls who do not mind will see a great deal of trouble. Come, let us go and see what you have done!"

They went down stairs, and found Mabel picking up the pieces, trying to see if she could fit them together so it could be mended.

"It is no use," said mama, upon seeing what she was doing, "for it is too badly broken to ever be mended. The pieces are very small!"

"What will we do with it?" Alice inquired.

"Just throw it out in the back lot on the ashes," replied mama.

So she swept up the pieces, carried the dustpan out and emptied it where her mother had told her to.

No sooner were the fragments thrown out than Speckle, the old rooster, came running up and began picking among them.

Alice saw he was actually swallowing some of the fine pieces, and was much alarmed.

She ran to the house and told her mama, who only laughed at her and explained that chickens need gravel, bits of crockery, and such things, to help them to chew their food.

"Well!" said Alice, "I should think it would kill him!"

"I will explain," replied mama, "the use of the gravel or crockery.

"They have no teeth to chew their food fine, ready for digestion; but inside of them are gizzards, or little tough bags, which hold the food after they swallow it.

"There needs to be something hard, like gravel or bits of crockery, to grind the food as the gizzard squeezes it.

"When I was a little girl, my little brother and I pounded up all the pieces of broken dishes, and threw them to the chickens, who were glad to get them."

"We will do that, and then the teapot will not be wasted, after all," said Alice.

Away ran the little girls, and a few minutes later, you might have seen them pounding the broken teapot into fine pieces on a large flat stone, while the

The Little Children love to read these Messages of Nature

chickens scrambled for the bits thrown to them.

That is what became of the teapot!

Modern Eve's Dress

The Bible relates how
In the days of yore,
Our dear wise Mother Eve
Very proudly wore

Her beautiful leaf-dress;
But if here today
A silk dress she could wear
In colors real gay.

The silkworm we would feed
On mulberry leaves,
'Till the soft strands of silk
He gallantly weaves.

Enough for a fine dress,
These workers, with skill,
Would in their industry,
Soon furnish the mill,

Where silk cloth and silk thread
  For dear *modern* Eve,
The looms, in a hurry,
  Would skilfully weave.

So the leaves of the trees
  In roundabout way,
Are worn by fair maidens
  In our modern day.

A Morning Talk About Cloth

WOOL

Children, what kind of a morning is this? Yes, a very cold morning. What did you like to wear? Overcoats, mittens, warm caps, and heavy suits and dresses are mentioned.

Of course we must dress warm when old Winter is here in earnest, to pinch our fingers and toes.

Of what are your caps and mittens made? That is right, of wool. Where do we get the wool? From the sheep, who is our little friend and helper.

A boy once told me he thought it cruel to take the wool from the sheep; but all

Winter, when he needed it to keep him warm, it was growing very thick.

When Spring came, it was not so comfortable for him, and in the hot Summer time, he wanted to get rid of it, and be cool again.

He soon finds that the farmer is his friend, and enjoys being washed, and having his wool cut off with the big shears.

This wool is sent to the mill to be made into cloth, yarn, and beautiful carpets, draperies and rugs for our homes!

Grandma knits the yarn into mittens for her little grandchildren.

Of what kind of cloth is John's coat made? Lucy's leggins? My dress?

Do you think we could do without woolen clothes for Winter?

Tomorrow you may bring any other kinds of cloth you can think of.

SILK

Here we are this morning, with samples of all kinds of cloth.

Children, what is this piece Mary has brought? "Silk." What is made from silk? Dresses, ties, gloves, handkerchiefs and many things are mentioned.

Do we get the silk from the sheep? Where do we get it? What do the little silkworms feed upon? Some day we will send for some silkworms, and you can then observe them day by day, care for them, and watch them work.

There are plenty of mulberry leaves to be found near by, and we will feed them and watch the little workers fasten themselves to twigs or leaves, by coarse threads, which they spin. They then curl up, and spin very fine silk threads all over their bodies. Soon they are inside their cocoons. The cocoon consists of three distinct layers of silk. The first is loose and soft, and can not be used by the silk manufacturer; the second is closer, and the third is still finer, and glued tightly together.

The cocoons must be watched carefully, and the silk wound off before the egress of the moth from its aurelian state.

We can tell when the caterpillar has passed into this state by shaking the cocoon, as the aurelia, from its hardened texture, will rattle. Then it is time to wind off the silk. This must be done before the chrysalis eats through the cocoon and spoils the silk. The cocoon is placed in a cup of warm water, after the loose silk on the outside has been removed, and then the end is taken, and the continuous filament is wound on a piece of card. It is now ready to be sent to the factory to be made into pretty ribbons and ties for you.

At first, China was the only country where silk was made, and at one time, a pound of it was worth a pound of gold.

After a while, it was introduced into India, and later, about the middle of the sixth century, two monks arrived at Constantinople, bringing eggs of the silkworm, and white mulberry, so they could raise them there. Soon they were raised in Italy, Spain, France and many parts of Europe.

We will talk about the rest of our samples another time.

LINEN

Here is a piece of cloth Charlie brought yesterday. What kind of cloth is it? Yes, it is linen. Do we get this from animals?

Then it is not an animal product, like the woolen and silk fabrics we have learned about. Where do we get it? That is right, it comes from a little plant called flax. It grows in the United States and many other countries.

The first linen cloth is said to have been manufactured in England in 1253 by the Flemish weavers. The stem of this plant is made up of little fibers, which, when separated from the woody outer covering of the stem, are called "lint." It is manufactured into cloth and thread.

The cloth is cool and makes nice Summer suits. Our table linen is also made from it. Can you name other uses?

The tiny flaxseeds are used for poultices, and from them, also, linseed oil is extracted. What is the oil used for?

The part of the seed left is not wasted, but made into oil cakes, which are very useful for feed for cattle and sheep.

Sometimes when these animals are caught in a great blizzard, the ranchman rides around among the suffering stock and feeds them these little oil cakes to keep up their strength.

COTTON

What kind of cloth has Tom brought?

Compare it with the wool, silk and linen we have been learning about. Is it like them? No, very different, as we see.

Where does the cotton come from?

I am holding up a picture of a pretty plant in bloom. It is the cotton plant, which is raised mostly in the South.

The fields are abloom in June, and look beautiful with their lovely flowers.

When the cotton ripens, we see a field of white stretching before us, reminding us of snow. When the pods burst, the cotton is ready to be gathered.

The bolls are full of seeds, and are removed by a machine called a cotton gin.

I have some cotton bolls which were brought to me by a friend from the South. I will hold them up and you may all look at them.

After the seeds are taken out, the cotton must be sent to the mill, where it is made into cloth and thread.

What is my apron made of? Nellie's dress? John's blouse?

Woolen, Silk, Cotton and Linen Cloth

The useful sheep I like the best,
He gives me wool to make my dress.
The tiny silkworm is good, too,
And spins silk strands so soft and new.

The cotton plant so strong does grow,
And fills with bolls as white as snow;
While little flax, with flowers so blue,
Grows to make *linen* cloth for you.

Seeing Good In Others

A lady's dresses hung in her closet in all their beauty.

There were robes of silk and wool, of cotton and linen. Party and street suits, kitchen dresses, and robes of all kinds, hung side by side in long rows.

Her great brown leather trunk sat in one corner of the closet, and as she traveled a great deal, and this was her favorite trunk, it was considered a better place for him, than to be stored away in the attic

with others of his cousins, who were seldom used.

Usually, quiet reigned in the closet home
of the dresses, but one day the silk dress
rustled noisily, as if to say, "I am the rich-
est dress here, and my lady loves me more
than any of the rest of you."

Then a fine woolen suit got prickly all
over, and replied: "How do you make that
out? She always chooses me on a cold day,
and I once heard her say that I had saved
her life many a time."

"Have you not seen," answered the silk-
en gown, "that she chooses me for all great
evening parties, or any gathering where
she cares to look beautiful?"

"Never mind about that," cried the linen
suit, "for it is I who gave her the most
comfort. In the hot summer days, she
wore me, instead of you, and called me her
'comfort' then."

"I think you are all wrong," said a simple cotton dress, from its dark corner.
"Have you not noticed how the lady comes
home, rushes upstairs, and takes you all
off in a hurry, as she says: "Now, let me

have my simple little wash dress, and then see about the supper.

"Then she puts me on, and can fly around with no fear of soiling a best dress, like you, who quarrel over your good looks.

"I heard her say that no matter what happened to me, I always laundered nicely, and was good as new again; but when anything happened to you, the rag-bag was almost certain to be your fate."

Now the old leather trunk had been listening to all of this, and he grew quite indignant to find that his companions could each be so self satisfied; and he was disgusted because they could not see the *good* in others, and only seem to see the good in themselves.

When he could stand it no longer, he talked until his straps were all loose. His preaching led them to see that each had its important place in the lady's wardrobe.

Presently they were startled by hearing their mistress and her maid come quickly into the room.

The closet door was thrown open, and if she noticed the dresses trembling, no doubt thought it was the wind from her sudden opening of the door. They heard her say: "Jane, won't you help me pull this trunk out, for I am going away to spend Christmas, and must pack it.

"As I am to remain sometime, I will have to take all kinds of dresses."

Then she took down nearly all of them. After they were snugly packed in her trunk, and she and Jane had left the room, the old trunk smiled as if to say:

"Well, I told you so!"

Studying Nature

Between the covers of a book
　　Nature's sweet story lingers,
While children quickly turn each page
　　With deft and nimble fingers.

The little doll, too, they must bring
　　That she may also listen.
I'm sure she really thinks it fine,
　　Just see how her eyes glisten!

The little children love to read
  These messages of Nature;
For flowers and trees and all such things
  Are sent to be their teacher.

In winter, when the flowers are gone,
  And birds have ceased their nesting,
Then turn they to their Nature Book
  And find it interesting.

The Lumbering Industry

We have already learned about the formation of coal, from the trees that flourished ages ago.

Now we will learn how the trees serve us many other ways.

In the northern part of the United States there are extensive forests.

The hard woods, as the oak, walnut, hickory, maple and ash are found in the colder countries. Maine is called the "Pine Tree State," because of its extensive pine forests. Soft woods come from the warmer climates.

Hard wood is very useful and durable.

Our ships, wagons, carriages, farm machinery, all kinds of furniture, interior woodwork, and floors, are made from it. You can think of many other uses, can you not?

The most extensively used wood of all is the white pine.

All of the section east of the Mississippi River was once a vast pine forest.

I will show you a picture of a pine forest.

When the early settlers came over here, they cut down these valuable trees, and instead of sending them to a lumber mill, they placed them in great piles and burned them; thus many acres of our large timber forests were wasted. Of some, they constructed log houses in which to live.

Now, the logs are sent to the lumber mills, to be made into boards and building material, of which our nice homes are built.

This illustrates the great progress and increasing intelligence of mankind.

We read a great deal now, about the conservation of the forests, which means, keeping or protecting from injury.

So many valuable forests have been destroyed by fires, that means must be taken to prevent this awful destruction and waste.

Michigan ranks first in the lumber industry, producing, it is estimated, about 5,000,000,000 feet of lumber yearly.

Minnesota and Wisconsin also produce vast quantities of lumber.

In the Winter time the lumbermen of the Northern forests begin their work.

This seems to be the best time, for there are then no leaves on the trees to hinder them; and the great logs can be easily hauled on sleds, to the river's bank, where they remain until the thawing of the ice in the Spring.

They are then guided down the stream to the mills, where they are sawed into boards.

The men guide the logs as they float and keep them from piling up.

They use a long pole with a point or hook at the end, to push them with.

Do you think the men who work in the cold, cutting down the trees, have good warm homes to stay in?

They build log houses, and a great many men live in these poor close quarters through the long cold winter.

Many of the men return year after year to their work, and their hardships only seem to make them stronger.

They call it a "logging camp."

I visited a lumber mill in Moline, Illinois, one evening.

The machinery was run by electricity, and was in operation both day and night.

One force of men worked all day, and when the six o'clock whistle blew for them to go home for their suppers, another force of men marched in, ready for the night's work.

At midnight a whistle told these men to stop and eat their lunches, and another, in the morning, told them to quit work and go home to rest in the daytime.

The noise was very deafening in the mill, and one would not care to venture in very far, among the vast amount of machinery, with its rapidly moving wheels and belts.

Do you not think it would be wonderful to see how quickly the boards, laths, and other materials for building, were turned out? Some friends once took me to visit a pine forest in Connecticut.

The trees were stately, tall and of such great circumference that they seemed to have flourished for ages.

Their fragrance was delightful, and the "singing of the pines" we had read about, now became real to us.

Near the edge of this pine forest, there was a camp meeting, which met every summer.

The little cottages nestled beneath the trees, making a pretty scene, as the stately monarchs of the forest towered above them, as if to protect them.

It was a beautiful sight, and left a mental picture never to be forgotten.

The old pines seemed to sing to us: "We know much about this country, and about the world, for we have been here a great many years."

PART THREE

SPRING

Looking for the first Bluebird

Spring Is Coming

Spring is coming, don't you know?
For a Robin told me so!
And a Blue Bird, blithe and gay,
Threw his song across the way,
Just to greet the little brook,
And the violets in their nook.

Sleeping flowers will wake and grow,
For the Robin told me so.
Now the sound of hoops we hear
And bright tops are spinning near,
Jumping ropes are all the go,
Boys and girls are glad, *we know.*

The Easter Talk

A beautiful Sunday is coming—called
"Easter Sunday."

This day comes at the time of year when
all is changing. The old is being made
new, and how happy every one is.

When Nature gives up the ice and snow,
the trees give up their long sleep, the seeds

burst into new life, and butterflies come forth from their dead appearing cocoons.

Everything seems to be proclaiming that death is life and "God is good."

The flowers say, "For a long time, we slept in seeds and bulbs, but we now come out into the bright, warm sunshine."

We adorn our churches with them, for in their silent beauty, they tell us the story of the resurrection.

They tell us that our bodies are the houses in which we live, and some day we will not need these houses any more, for in a new life, we will be made more beautiful in our home in heaven.

We love to sing:
"Waken sleeping butterfly!
    Burst your narrow prison;
Spread your golden wings and rise
    For the Lord is risen.
Spread your wings and tell the story
How he arose—the Lord of Glory."

Furry Little Caterpillar

Furry little caterpillar
　　Crawling near my garden walk,
Furry, sleepy caterpillar,
　　Would you tell, if you could talk,

How you spin your silken cocoon,
　　Where you're safe from prying eye,
And when comes the gladsome spring time
　　You come out a butterfly?

Never talking, always dreaming,
　　Of the time when you will pause,
To trade off your little fur-coat,
　　For those lovely wings of gauze!

Then, instead of crawling, living,
　　On leaves of cabbages and weed,
You will flit among the blossoms,
　　Sipping honey for your feed!

The Caterpillar

Children, let us look at this queer little thing with its fur coat. It is not as large as your thumb, and is called a "caterpillar." Its name, when written on the board, as you see, is as long as he is.

Its fur is black, brown and yellow, and it has ten short legs and ten little feet.

Six of the feet are provided with fine hooks which he uses for tools. His jaws are very strong, and in his head is a little machine which is called a "spinnerette."

He has six black eyes and can see ten inches away, so it is said, but no farther.

He lives in trees and travels up and down the branches.

He eats a great deal and is eating most of the time. Leaves and buds are his favorite food. When eating, he twists himself into a knot and holds the leaf in the hooks of his feet while he bites it off.

He keeps on eating and growing, often bursting his coat and getting a new one. After this has happened many times, he is as large as he ever will be, when he begins to have queer feelings. The funny machine in his head begins to work and he becomes cold, sleepy and dizzy. He wants a warm coat. Then the machine spins yards and yards of fine soft thread, until his little house is all finished, and he is in the inside of it, ready for a long sleep. He sleeps until spring comes with its warm days, and at the proper time he is awakened.

He opens his eyes and creeps slowly from his silken house; but he hardly knows himself, for instead of the old fur suit he went to sleep in, he has a beautiful suit, as fine as velvet.

Instead of ten feet, he now has six active little limbs, and beautiful, richly tinted wings. His eyes are like diamonds, and he can see far away.

Now he does not care for leaves to eat, but likes honey from the flowers.

He does not know, even, what he is, until some children exclaim:

"Oh, see that lovely butterfly!"

When night comes, he folds his wings and creeps into some dainty flower cup.

He always did his work well, and did his very best. Do you not think he deserved his rest?

He came out from his deep sleep into a more glorious life, reminding us of the Easter time.

The Butterfly Talk

Butterflies are the most beautiful of all insects.

On account of the feather like scales of which their wings are covered, and to which their rare coloring is due, they are technically called, "Lepidoptera," meaning scale winged insects.

We will hold this one up, and look at it. Now count its wings. There are four, two large, and two smaller ones, which it spreads when flying. They are covered with beautiful down which is easily rubbed off. So we see, they are not made to be handled. Many a little boy has caught the beautiful butterfly he was chasing, and after he had touched it, could see the marks of his fingers, where they had taken off the soft down.

The body, which is long and slender, is placed between the wings and covered with fine hairs. It has six legs which are used for standing.

Upon the head are two long horns which are knotted at each end. He now has two eyes and four feelers. How many eyes did he have when he was a caterpillar?

He can now see *far away*. Could he then?

The mouth is a long, hollow trunk, placed between two of the feelers.

With it, he sips the honey from flowers. When not in use, the tube is kept curled up.

Now we will let our little pet go, for he wants his freedom, and we must not be cruel to any living thing.

Blue Bird

My darling little Blue Bird,
   Singing in the tree,
Oh, what is the lovely song
   That you sing to me?

Flying through the branches high
   Showing colors gay,
Now, tell me, pretty Blue Bird,
   What is this you say?

I hear his sweet clear answer:
   "'Tis of Spring I tell,
And of our loving Father,
   Who made all things well.

"I've come to chase the sorrow
   From the aching heart,
And fill the world with gladness,
   This is now my part."

Pussy Willows

Why worry, little pussy coats?
You know the warm Spring sun will come,
And kiss each little dainty crib
Which all the winter was your home.

And the sunbeams warm will hurry,
And make ice and snow all scurry!
They'll call you out to greet the dawn,
You pussies dear, so fat and warm!

Alice and the Leaves

It was a beautiful May day, and little Alice was taking a walk under the old apple tree which grew in her yard.

She looked up, and saw the beautiful green leaves of the tree, which made such a nice cool dress for it. Little birds sang in the branches, and the leaves gladly curtained off the nests, and shaded the eyes of the baby birds from the bright sunlight.

It was a wonderful picture to Alice, who had been sick a part of the Winter and Spring, and not able to be out of doors for some time.

She looked up, and said: "Oh, you pretty leaves! When I last saw the tree, it was brown and bare. Where *did* you all come from?"

All the leaves nodded, as though glad to see her, and some of them rustled as if to welcome their little friend. She caught one low branch in her hand, and picked off what she thought was the prettiest leaf, a very large one, which she called the "mama leaf"; then she took off the smallest, which she called the "baby leaf."

She sat down under the tree, for she was very tired, the walk from her swing near the house having been longer than she thought it would be.

Alice turned the leaves over in her hands, and noticed how much the baby looked like the mamma. The dresses were both trimmed the same way around the edges. They were both velvety and soft, and had a fine network of veins. They had slender stems which had held them to the twig.

Alice said: "Now, I think this large leaf is old enough to tell me all about itself and little brother and sister leaves."

Then she leaned back and closed her eyes, but the leaf did nothing for some time.

When Alice had sat quite still a few minutes, the leaf rustled and tried to sing, as leaves will, sometimes, in the wind; and this is what it was telling her:

"The tree has sent you a message, that you can find out all about the little leaf children by calling at the Elm tree that grows a few yards distant.

"Our mother is busy getting the apples ready for the children, and our neighbor, the Elm, who lives near, has no fruits or nuts to prepare."

Then Alice visited the Elm tree, and the little elm leaf children were just as glad to see her as were the little apple leaf children.

She asked the mother Elm to tell her about the leaves, where they came from, and what they were for.

The kind old tree replied: "Indeed, we trees love little children. Do you not see what fine large branches I am sending forth to shade you and your little friends? Well, in the Autumn, when it grew cold, I took good care of my little baby buds, and gave them winter clothes to keep them warm; for they were to open into leaves in the Spring. The outside coat was a gum coat to keep the rain off. With their little warm coats about them, they slept through the cold weather, rocked in their cradles by the wind, and caring nothing for Jack Frost.

"After their winter nap, when the warm winds and sunbeams brought their loving message from the Heavenly Father, they began to move in their cradles; and swell, little by little, until they burst their winter coats, which they would not need any more. People walked under the branches and said: 'The leaves are budding.' In a short time, my branches were dressed in lovely green, and I am sure I am proud of my little leaf children. They are the *best* children I ever saw."

"What can they do?" inquired Alice.

"I will tell you," said the tree; "but first let me show you a leaf, and tell you about the different parts of it. This large part of the leaf is the blade, one face of which looks up at the sky, and one down to the earth. This leaf is made of two kinds of material, the green pulp, and the fibrous framework, or skeleton, which supports the soft, green pulp, making the leaf firm and strong. This framework is a woody material, which runs from the stem through the leaf stalk.

"In the blade of the leaf, these spread out and form the ribs and veins.

"The large part of the leaf drinks in air and sunshine. Without these, the tree would not thrive, and would soon die.

"After this, when you look at trees, you will know that they breathe through their leaves, just as little children breathe through their lungs."

"How funny!" said Alice. "Thank you very much for your story, dear tree."

As the Elm reminded Alice that black clouds were gathering, and she had better hurry home, she ran off as fast as she could, but she heard the leaves singing, "It is going to rain, and now the dust will be washed off so we can breathe better, and gather in more sunshine."

Then Alice felt some one shaking her, and rubbed her eyes, and looked up, to see her mama, who wanted her to come to supper.

Little Pussy Willow

Pleasant is the Springtime—
  For on every bough,
Pretty little Pussies
  All are nodding now.

Tell me, little Pussies,
  When it's cold and bleak,
Why within your houses,
  You so snugly sleep?

"Oh we know the Winter
  Soon will go away;
Then we'll gently rouse us,
  And come out and play."

'Tis the warm sun tells us
  When it's time to stir,
And come peeping at you
  In our coats of fur."

How funny, little Pussies!
  We put *our* furs away,
When *you* are just appearing,
  In furs all dressed so gay!

Linnaeus

Children, you love to see and gather the lovely flowers around you, and when older, you will study Botany and learn about the families to which they belong, and many things very interesting.

I must tell you about Linnaeus, who did so much for the study of Botany. He was born in Sweden, May 13, 1707.

Although his parents were very poor, he was always happy among the weeds and flowers. It has been said of him, that he began to study Botany as soon as he could see, and at the age of four years, he asked his father questions about the weeds, flowers and plants.

His father, who was a minister, wanted his son to become one, too, and finally sent him to a school to receive this preparation, but he failed to become interested in his studies, and was called a "dunce."

His teachers said he could never make a minister or scholar of any kind, as he was so dull. They thought he had no mind at all. He was sent to other schools, but none of his teachers could cure his craving for plant study, and make him like school.

He procured books by the few Swedish authors who had written of plant life, and these he studied with great delight. He cared for nothing but Botany and Biology.

When Linnaeus was seventeen years old, his teachers told his father to make a tailor or shoemaker of the boy, as he was too dull to ever be anything else. This grief and disappointment was hard to bear, and he told his old friend, Dr. Rothman, of his son's failure.

Dr. Rothman was able to see something deeper than the making of a tradesman of this dull boy; therefore he offered to board him for the year left in his school course.

This new found friend gave Linnaeus lessons in Physiology, and instructed him in the best system of Botany then obtainable.

When he was twenty years old, he went to the University of Lund, where he lived with a learned man who had a museum of minerals, plants, birds and shells, which he greatly delighted in.

At night he read books on Natural History, so you see the boy who had been considered dull, could study subjects for which he had talent.

Of course his development was now very rapid; but he was influenced to leave and go to Upsala, where he could have better advantages.

At this time, he had less than fifty dollars in his pocket, and had no hopes of getting more from his father, who was a poor minister. Yet he thought best to go, and as he was a stranger, he could make nothing by teaching.

His small sum of money was soon gone, and he spent a year in great adversity, thankful for even one meal a day.

His shoes became thin and ragged and he mended them himself, as best he could.

An old minister, who had noticed his deep study of plants, became acquainted with him. He could see deeper than the rags of Linnaeus' clothing, and thought him a great student, rarely gifted.

This new friend was Olaf Celsius, a professor of theology.

He was writing his "Hierobotanicon" at
this time, and invited Linnaeus to his
home. He saw his collection of plants, and
considered his explanations of them wonderful, so he asked Linnaeus to make his
home with him. This was surely good
fortune for the poor young man, and he
soon began to write his book on the sexes
of plants.

Prof. Rudbeck was so delighted with
this, that he wanted him for his assistant.
Thus Linnaeus was now reveling among
his flowers like a happy butterfly. He gave
lectures and published many books. I have
not time to tell you of all of them, but we
must notice his "Genera Plantarum," for
it is considered the beginning of the natural system of Botany.

At the age of thirty-two, he was mar-
ried, and a year later Prof. Rudbeck died,
and Linnaeus became a professor in the
University at Upsala, where he had once
been the starving student.

Everything was praise and glory for
him now. Kings sought him and the Uni-
versities all wanted him; but he preferred
to remain there, and kept on writing other

botanical works. The school became so popular that in a short time the attendance was trebled.

He died in the year 1778.

Before Linnaeus' time plants were not studied much except as foods or medicines.

There may be some boy or girl who finds it difficult to like school as they should, and who are considered dull by their teachers and parents. Let them be told the story of Linnaeus, and they will be encouraged to persevere, that their minds, like his, may develop in time, in the right way.

Planting the Seed

In our little flowerbed
  We have just made anew,
We plant the seed so small
  That it may grow for you.

There, in the fresh, rich soil,
  Warmed by the Spring sunshine,
The little seed will swell,
  And soon become a vine.

The rains have given it
  The moisture it will need.
Soon two cotyledons
  Are bursting from the seed.

The root is growing, too;
  And will take from the ground
The foods and juices good,
  That in its work are found.

The stem shoots up and up,
  And, when it's time for them,
Some more leaves will burst forth
  To make us glad again.

And on it proudly grows
  With all its little might.
Soon *buds* are bursting forth
  To fill us with delight.

Some morning we will go
  To see this little vine,
And blossoms we will find
  That in the sun do shine.

In the green calyx bright
    Our pretty flower rests.
The lovely corolla
    Little bees love, I guess.

They sip the pure honey
    And quietly settle,
As if they were owners
    Of each fair soft petal.

The Hen and the Turkey

One warm day in April, little brown leghorn hen, who was called "Brownie," strolled through the gate to see if the bugs and seeds she liked best, would not taste better on the other side of the fence.

She was very dainty and particular about what she had to eat. Besides, there could be no danger of visiting outside the yard occasionally, as she always found her way back.

Then, too, the farmer had said that very morning, "that she would soon be ready to be set."   She knew that meant no running around for *three* weeks, at least.

So she picked up bits of sweet green grass, little bugs and insects, kernels of corn that had been dropped; and soon forgot that she had strolled away from the rest of the chickens and was walking around quite alone.

Pretty soon a little boy came along, swinging a bright new tin pail in his hand,

and amused himself by trying to make her run.

She was much frightened, and ran a long way, and was soon farther from home than she had intended to go.

When she stopped, she found herself in the long grass, and right before her, on a nest, was a large turkey.

The turkey looked *very* much surprised, and the hen stared at her and wondered what strange bird it was; for her master kept no turkeys, and she had never seen one before.

When she had gotten her breath, she said: "Did I frighten you?" "No," said the turkey. "I am used to hens like you, for there are a great many living at the same place with me. I come out here so they won't know where my nest is, and now I hope you won't tell anybody, because if you do, my eggs might be taken. I am a turkey, and turkeys never want the people to know where their nests are. That is why we make them in the long grass."

Little Brownie said "she would never tell, but she didn't see how a turkey could bear to leave a nice home in the barn-

Blossoms we will find

yard, where there were nests in boxes and barrels, fixed on purpose for them."

Just then, the turkey came off the nest, and instead of cackling like a hen does, to let all the neighbors know she had laid an egg, she stole stealthily away, and whispered to the hen, "to come on, before any one should see them."

But Brownie paused and looked curiously at the large speckled egg, so unlike her own. "There are several in the nest. Sometime you will have some nice little chickens," said the hen.

"No, of course not! Turkeys they will be," replied Mrs. Turkey. "What do you think," said Brownie, "I didn't know whether you would hop or walk when you came off the nest. I have noticed birds that walk, just as I do, and many that hop." Then the wise turkey told her "that all walking birds have strong legs and toes, and hopping birds have slender legs and small toes. All the barnyard fowls have legs and feet, made for walking.

Then she mentioned the guinea hens, peacocks, ducks, geese, turkeys, hens and pigeons; also quails who do not live in the barnyard.

The turkey, who was very clever at telling the time of day by her shadow, said "she must be going home." So they bade each other "good-by," and the little hen went down the road to the gate.

Some one had closed it while she was gone, but she was very lively and crawled under the fence. Soon she was with the other fowls in the barnyard, who told her how much they missed her, for she was a great favorite.

The warm Spring days came and went, until the little hen was about five weeks older than when this story began. She was put in a coop in which she was securely fastened, but was not alone; for there were twelve little chickens, in warm, soft downy coats, running around. How proud she was, and how much she had taught them!

They all loved each other very much, and were a happy little family.

Brownie thought she would have to take another stroll down the road, and see how her turkey friend was getting along.

Besides, she was so proud of her chicks
that she wanted her friend to see them.
Then she was sure they were all doing fine-
ly, and would soon be so large and strong,
that the farmer would let them out to run
around on the farm.

One morning she was made very happy
by being let out as she had wished, and
seeing the gate open, she called her chicks
and stole cautiously away. The hen was
glad to be able to walk down the road
again, for it was her favorite walk, and
she knew she would see the turkey not far
away. The little chicks did not get tired,
as they were quite strong, and their mother stopped every now and then to let them
rest.

But she had to go every step of the way
to the long grass before seeing the turkey.
Mrs. Turkey was very busy at home with
a fine family of little turkeys.

"How do you do?" said Brownie. "I
have brought my dear little chickens to see
you."

"I am very glad," said the turkey, "for
I was just wishing you could see what a

nice family I have, after sitting on my eggs just *four weeks!*"

"*Four weeks?*" said Brownie, "why, I only had to stay on the nest *three weeks!*"

"Yes," said Mrs. Turkey, "but hens and turkeys are not much alike, and how does it come that you take them so far from home when they are so young? Now my little ones are *very* weak, and have to be taken care of. They can't stand the wet at all, and I expect the farmer will be here soon to put them in a safer, drier place."

Just then the farmer came, and the little hen thought she had better be going, so they said "Good-by."

Brownie was greatly satisfied that she had chicks to raise instead of delicate little turkeys.

Spring Rain

Patter, patter, gentle rain,
Come to tell of Spring again.
Come to bring us fragrant flowers
That will brighten Summer hours.

Then search for the Daisy's Secret, my Darling Little One

Patter, patter, drip-drip-drip!
Give the pretty birds a sip.
Fill the little lambkins' trough,
See them drink and scamper off!

Reading the Flowers

What does my darling little one
  Read in the flowers so fair?
Methinks she's reading in their depths
  That Nature's God is there.

We see it in the sunset bright,
  We read it in the skies;
And every night we find 'tis true,
  Told in the stars' bright eyes.

And in the mountain scenery
  Or in the waterfall,
We hear the lovely story true,
  That "God is All in all."

Then search for the daisy's secret,
  My darling little one.
In every lovely plant that blooms
  Great truths will be made known.

Uncle George's Story of the Birds

"The first bird I will tell you about," said Uncle George, "is the European Sparrow. He is a bold bird, and goes to the pigeon houses, and with his sharp beak, opens the crops of young pigeons, then eats the half-digested grain.

"He finds this an easy way to get his food, so is lazy as well as cruel.

"They annoy the farmers by eating so much grain, but they also help him, by ridding the land of insects.

"A pair of sparrows destroy for their little family over 3,360 caterpillars in a week.

"They are easily tamed and will hop around the house. I once cut some meat in small pieces and they liked it immensely.

"You would like to know, too, about the little song sparrows, some of whom remain all Winter.

"If wounded and unable to fly, they can swim. They build their nests on the ground under tufts of grass. Their nests

are made of horsehair and dried grass.
Sometimes they build in cedar trees. They
are six and a half inches long, and a dark
chestnut color, marked with white. The
breasts are spotted.

"Now I must tell you about the Parrot,
for you have seen many of them. He has
brilliant plumage, of green or green and
red, and can imitate the human voice, for
he has a fleshy, thick tongue. Some can
speak distinctly and whistle, sing and
laugh. One that I heard, said: 'Don't make
me cry so; I shall die!' He could mew like
a cat, and bark like a dog, also whistle for
the dog.

"Some of them eat seeds of plants, fruit
and grain. The wild ones roost in hollow
trees, and lay their eggs on a few pieces of
rotten wood at the bottom.

"I once knew a man who had a parrot
he bought while in Europe, and as he traveled, he taught it several languages.

"He brought it to this country and at
the time I saw this lovely bird, its home
was in St. Louis. It often picked pieces of
wood from the parlor furniture, when let
out for exercise. They are very fond of

pretty things, and most always peck at precious stones set in rings or pins. Another quite large bird which you may have seen is the Owl."

Owls

"Owls prowl about at night and kill animals which are asleep.

"Their flight is noiseless, as the wings are soft and downy. Like others birds of prey, they have hooked beak and claws.

"They have a funny habit of bowing awkwardly to each other, and are short and chunky with eyes set far in front. Their eyes are sensitive to sunlight, and if in a bright light, roll their eyes as if in pain. They are made for seeing in the dark. The legs, feet and bills are covered with feathers, so they can hardly be seen.

"They make their homes in hollow trees, sometimes stealing the squirrels' nests. Some have nests in old buildings.

"Do you not think the farmers are glad to have them eat so many mice which hurt their grain? I once visited in the country and saw a young owl about half grown, which a man found and brought home to his little girl. She set him up on the fence in the bright sunlight, and he rolled his eyes and made a terrible noise.

"She fed him a small ground squirrel which had been caught in a trap. He swallowed it whole, bones, hairy coat, and all. After it had been down a short time he threw up the bones, skin and all undigestible parts. The little girl laughed, and told him 'he had better dress his meat before eating it,' but that is not his way.

"He is called a *wise* bird, perhaps because he holds himself with such dignity and always has a very wise expression.

"Now we have heard about the sparrows, parrots and owls, and must go to supper.

"Tomorrow I will tell you about some other birds."

Birds So Gay

If I were but a little bird
    Just like you,
I'd throw away my little dress,
    And wear blue.

Then in my pretty feather coat
    I'd fly high.
I'd touch the clouds so soft and white
    In the sky.

Tell me, my little songster gay,
    Why are you
On every day and Sundays too
    Dressed in blue?

And why such little dainty feet
    That can hop;
And when you're happy you just sing,
    And never stop?

Robins, Blue Birds and Blue Jays

One evening, as the children sat around the fire, Teddie reminded Uncle George that he must finish telling him about the birds. Uncle, seeing it was Ted's way never to forget a promise, began:

"When I was a boy, the Robin was my favorite bird, so I will tell you about him first. He spends the Winter in South Carolina and returns to us in March. He builds his nest in a fork of the old apple tree, plasters it with mud, and lines it with fine grass.

"Mother Robin lays about five eggs of a bluish green color.

"They eat worms, berries and caterpillars. Sometimes they line their nests with fine shavings, or soft feathers. They are quite tame and will come to bushes and take threads, hair and anything suitable if the children place it there for them, and weave it into their nests.

"I must now tell you of our earliest messenger of Spring, the

BLUE BIRD

"Sometimes he returns in February. If possible, they like to repair their nest of the former year's building. If this cannot be done, they set diligently to work to make a new home.

"Soon, five or six light blue eggs are laid, of which they are quite proud.

"During the Spring and Summer their song is a beautiful warbling, which changes in October to a single plaintive note.

"The male is six and three-fourths inches long, with full broad wings.

"The upper parts are of a rich sky blue, reflecting some purple.

"He is called 'A harbinger of Spring,' because he returns so early. I am sure he is looking for the little boys and girls he used to see last Spring; and for the return of the early flowers—the Spring beauties —violets and tulips.

The little boys and girls are looking for him, too; and no doubt he thinks them little Spring beauties, as they eagerly gaze into the treetops, looking for the first bluebird.

"Now I will tell you about a bird which is very pretty to look at, but when you become acquainted with him, you learn that he is selfish and mean.

"I am telling you about the

BLUE JAY

"I dislike to have anything bad to tell about any of our little birds, but I cannot give you a description of this one without relating a few of his mean traits. He is very beautiful to look at, but we all remember the saying: 'Fine feathers do not make fine birds.'

"You have all seen him, with his pretty plumage and crested head, and have noticed his broad wings, and tail, which is banded with blue, black, and white.

"He likes to taste eggs other birds have laid, and drives them off their nests, sometimes hurting them badly. He even devours the young birds and attacks disabled animals.

"The Blue Jay stores surplus food away in some hole in a tree or crack in the bark. He is so greedy that he will eat all he can, and then hide the food remaining from other birds.

"He is a great enemy of the owl.

"Now," said Uncle George, "I must read my paper, but I will tell you some other day of the swallows, orioles, and woodpeckers, for we often hear little Lucy sing the song she learned at kindergarten, about them."

The Nest Builders

Times are not dull in the woodland,
  As the busy workers there
Are hammering and plastering,
  Building their new homes with care.

There Woodpecker, with his hammer
  Is busy the live long day;
And the Swallow, with his plaster,
  Is at work across the way.

And the gay Oriole weaver
  Will make the hammocks so fine,
While our frisky Mr. Squirrel
  Is watching him all the time.

Now these busy wildwood dwellers
  Never talk about their pay,
Since He who cares for the lilies
  Is feeding them every day.

The Swallow, Oriole and Woodpecker

Lucy was singing her song, "The Swallow is a Mason," when Uncle George said: "That song reminds me of my promise, so sit down, children, and I will tell you about the Swallow, Oriole and Woodpecker."

They were very glad Uncle George had remembered his promise, and soon, four little chairs were drawn up and eight bright eyes were eagerly watching for him to begin: "You know, for the little song teaches it, that birds have trades, the same as men have.

"The little Swallow is a fine mason, as you see, when you look at this nest," said uncle, holding up a swallow's nest. "See how beautifully it is plastered. The swallow's trowel is his bill, his mortar is mud, made firm with fine hay and the glutinous saliva of the bird. With mud and hay and leaves he makes his comfortable little nest.

The Chimney Swallows live in chimneys of the farm houses.

"The Barn Swallows' plumage is beautifully mixed with blue-black on the upper parts, and rich fawn or drab color below. The tail is deeply forked, the two outer feathers being nearly twice the length of the others.

"The Chimney Swallows are a plain mouse color, the tail nearly even, and each feather ending in a sharp point.

"The Swallows are very neighborly and sociable. When they go South in Winter, they go in great companies.

"A gentleman was once traveling when he came to a forest, through which he was obliged to pass, and as a severe storm came up he decided to rest under the shelter of a fine old tree. In the early morning he was startled by the terrific roaring which seemed to come from within the trunk. He placed his ear to the tree, and the noise became very loud. Soon a large company of Swallows flew out and were followed by so great a number it would have been impossible to count them. The gentleman knew they were seeking a warmer climate and had gone into the hollow tree to pass the night and rest for the next day's journey."

"Do they always travel in large companies?" asked Teddie. "Yes," said Uncle George. "Twenty or thirty nests are often seen in the same barn, so you may know they like neighbors, and no doubt have good times visiting.

"The Swallow lays five eggs, which are white, with reddish brown spots.

"They raise two broods in a season, and the last leave their nest about the first week in August.

"When the young are fledged, the parents coax them out of their nests to exercise their wings in the barn.

"Swallows eat insects, which they catch on the wing. Now we have heard about the *mason,* and I must tell you about the weaver, or the

ORIOLE

"This beautiful singer, with lovely black and orange plumage, weaves a little bag of grass, bark and wool, strengthened with pieces of strings and hair.

"His little nest would remind you of a hammock, as he hangs it from a strong twig, fastening it firmly.

"The farmer thinks he is a great helper, as he rids the orchards of worms.

"He is called the 'Baltimore Oriole,' because his colors were those of Lord Baltimore, formerly proprietary of Maryland.

"Some of the birds are better workers than others, and make smoother, stronger nests.

"They often carry off the thread which has been put out to bleach.

"Our little friend is seven inches long, with head, throat, upper parts of back and wings black.

"The lower part of the back and whole under parts are bright orange.

"The tail is black and orange.

"If you are not too tired, I will tell you about the carpenter, or

WOODPECKER

"His food consists of insects and their eggs, which are deposited beneath the bark of decayed trees.

"He is supplied with a large hammer-shaped head, and long, sharp bill. By their aid, he strips away the bark, and gets his food. If insects are beneath the bark, he uses his long tongue, which is barbed at the end and can be protruded beyond the beak.

"With his bill he also digs out of the tree a hole in which to raise his young. This hole is often three feet in depth, and sometimes much less. His legs are short and muscular, and the toes are placed two before and two behind, so he can take hold of the bark firmly.

"Now we have learned about all the little birds of Lucy's song," said Uncle. "Yes," replied Lucy, "and it sounds like our kindergarten stories, too."

A Dream Poem

A Swallow worked hard for seven days,
Having no time for visits or plays,
And built her nest of mud, hay and leaves,
Right under the old brown stone house
    eaves.

The nest was finished, and she was proud,
And sang her songs very clear and loud:
"My home is the nicest in the land!
Happy we'll be in our nest so grand."

Two boys who lived in the brown stone
    house,
Crept out as still as a little mouse;
And climbed the ladder so straight and tall,
And carried away the nest so small.

"Now, I'd like to know who owns this
    place?"
Said one little boy, with pouting face.
"Our father does, and the nest is ours,
'Though the swallows worked at it for
    hours."

"'Tis ours, of course! It belongs to us.
Those swallows need not make such a
      fuss!"
Then they carried it to their own room,
And the swallows' joy was turned to
      gloom.

Then sadly they sang, from day to day,
For their home had been carried away.
"We'll build another in the same place
In spite of the boy with pouting face."

The kind neighbor birds all came to see
If they could not all of them agree
To hold a meeting at half past one
To see if something could not be done.

So Robins, Sparrows and Thrushes, too,
Woodpeckers, Orioles, and Bird Blue,
Met in a row on the old clothesline,
And argued 'til nearly half past nine.

Finally, they decided 'twas best
To *buy* the house, if they built the nest.
"We'll give a fine concert," said Bird Blue,
"And earn some money to help us through."

The boys heard all that the birds had said,
And with faces sad and hearts like lead,
They resolved never again to take
A nest which the little birds should make.

A Morning Talk About Birds
PART ONE
Give, each week, as much as the children
are ready for.

Birds build their nests in the Spring, so
their little ones, who are bare, will have
the warm sun to shine on them.   Then,
too, food is easily found in Spring and
Summer, and with good food and plenty of
warmth, they will grow strong by Fall,
and be able to fly about for food, and to go
South when it is too cold for them here.

The different birds build their nests near
the kind of food they eat.   That is, the
sparrows, swallows and thrushes, build
near houses, as the flies and insects they
like are to be found there.

· The storks build near ponds, because
they like frogs.

Woodpeckers hunt decayed trees, where
they can get the insects they are so fond of.

Tomorrow, we will have some real nests and pictures of nests to look at.

Each bring one, if you can, and tell us something about it.

PART TWO

Who can tell me where our birds who are *scratchers,* spend most of their time? What do they eat? Where do they roost? They eat seeds, insects, grains, etc. They have heavy bodies, short wings, and legs of moderate length and size. Their toes are straight, and nails short and blunt.

Their three front toes are the longest, and united near the leg by a membrane. The hind toe is short, and placed high on the leg.

Their young are hatched with their eyes open, and are generally able to run about for their food as soon as they are out of the shell.

PART THREE

Who can mention some of our swimmers? Yes, the ducks, geese, and swans belong to this class. The toes of swimming birds are joined by a web or skin, which makes them nice little oars.

Their bodies are boat-shaped, which enables them to move more easily through the water. Their legs are short and placed far back under their bodies, which makes them very good swimming paddles; but when walking about on land they are very awkward.

Their thick plumage is packed underneath with down, while the outside feathers overlap each other, and are kept well oiled. Thus, you see, the skin does not become wet from the water in which they swim. They reach down into the pond with their long necks and get their food.

How do the ducks strain their food? What kind of bills do they have?

All bring pictures of ducks and other swimming birds tomorrow.

A Talk About Perchers

Have you ever seen a little bird sitting on a tree? How does he hold on so nicely without falling?

The perchers have four toes, two front and two back ones. Their legs and feet are slender. Their wings are long and quite large, enabling them to be great flyers. You may name some of our perchers. The children name robins, orioles, sparrows, canaries, and any they may have noticed.

Bring pictures of perchers tomorrow. and if possible, bring a canary bird.

Lead the children to be kind to the birds. and to scatter crumbs for those who remain with us for the Winter.

Teach them to place water where they can reach it, and if very cold, snowy weather, to tie suet to the branches of the trees, that they may have heat producing food. Encourage humane treatment of all their pets, both birds and animals.

CLASSES OF BIRDS.

- Scratchers and walkers }Types{ Chickens, Pigeons, Turkeys, Guinea-hens, etc.
- Perchers and those that hop and chirp }Types{ Sparrows, Swallows, Canaries, Blue-birds, Orioles, etc.
- Climbers }Types{ Woodpecker, Parrots
- Talkers }Type{ Parrot
- Swimmers }Types{ Ducks, Geese, Swans
- Robbers or Birds of Prey }Types{ Eagles, Hawks
- Waders }Type{ Stork
- Runners }Type{ Ostrich

The Wren and Brown Thrush

"Oh, Uncle," cried Lucy, "our cat has caught a little bird, and I fear she will eat it!" "I will see if I can get it away from her," said uncle; but it was too late. Pussy had really devoured the tiny bird, and nothing but the feathers strewn about on the grass could show that little wren had ever existed.

"I wish, Uncle George, you would tell me all about the wrens," said Lucy. "All right," replied the good-natured uncle. "Sit down near me, and I will tell you a short story:

"The wren comes back to us in April, and builds a nest in the wooden cornice under the eaves, or in a hollow cherry tree. They prefer small boxes nailed on top of a post in the garden, or to the side of the house, near the eaves. I once knew of an old brick building, and the wrens built nests in the little holes where some of the bricks had crumbled out. Some have made their nests in an old hat, nailed up, with a little place left for their door.

"One time a workman hung his coat up under a shed. Two or three days passed before he put it on, and then, as he was putting one arm in the sleeve, he found it filled with old leaves, paper, grass and hair. He started to pull the rubbish out, and found a wren's nest. They flew around him, scolding, as if to let him know they thought he had done wrong to destroy their nest. They like to hop on the ground near the houses, but are in great danger as the cat is very fond of these little birds.

"They are of a dark brownish color, and remind me of our little brown thrush!"

"I would like to hear about the brown thrushes," said Lucy, "for I know a song about them."

"Well," continued uncle, "he is just a little bit larger than a robin, with reddish brown plumage on his back. The under parts are of a yellowish color, spotted with brown. The tail is very long, and their song is loud and varied in tone. He is one of our finest musicians, and if half a mile away, we could hear his song.

"He builds his nest early in May, sometimes in a vine, but prefers the hedge or thorn bush. There is a brown thrush's nest in our grapevine which I must show you. It is constructed of tiny sticks, pieces of fine roots, and dry leaves. He has a very strong bill, and if the blacksnake molests his nest, he attacks it and protects his little family.

"He eats worms, beetles, grubs, berries, and caterpillars. They are quite tame and fly low, spreading their tails out like a fan.

"Now you have learned about two of our tamest little birds, and I must go to my work," said Uncle George.

Froebel

Be glad and sing, little children,
  For one was born this day,
Who wrote us lovely songs,
  And taught little children to play.

Now we can be pretty fishes,
  Or trains of cars that run;
Snails crawling into shells,
  Or prancing ponies full of fun.

We are happy while we're at school,
  And happy when at play.
We love our pretty work,
  Whether 'tis sewing, mats or clay.

Oh, what would we do, dear Froebel,
  Throughout this world today,
Had you not planned for us,
  Education through work and play.

The Evolution of the Apple

Have you noticed how Mother Nature gets the apples ready for the children?

If we visit the orchard, we will find many trees with their great branches loaded with buds.

These will be very small at first, and all enclosed in their little green jackets.

The days grow warmer all the time, and soon the buds become larger, and show a little pink color peeping out of their door. They will gradually unfold until we see many larger buds, and finally, the tree is filled with the full blown apple blossoms, whose perfume and beauty make everyone glad.

After these lovely blossoms have adorned the trees for a short time, their petals begin to fall, and all over the ground, beneath the trees, they form a soft carpet.

Looking up, we see the little blossom stems, with the green calyx which had held the flower. How many there are! These will grow and grow, until you will see the calyces forming into little green apples.

The sepals, as the tiny green parts of the calyx are called, will sometime become the blow of the apple.

Some apples mature early, while others grow larger and larger all summer, and are not ready to be gathered until Fall.

These are our Winter apples. The apple trees have enemies who come to destroy the fruit, and if not gotten rid of in time, many apples are ruined.

These enemies are the worms, who are very fond of apples.

We do not like to find wormy fruit on our trees.

A way has been discovered to spray the trees and get rid of the pests, and very nice fruit is being raised. This fine perfect fruit sells for better prices than poor fruit.

In some States, Montana for instance, there are district inspectors who are required to visit and spray all local orchards; and they are empowered to destroy an entire fruit district, if it should prove necessary to get rid of a pest.

You may bring apple seeds, and we will plant them and watch them grow

Potato Planting

Little Edith went to the country
    To visit her grandpa one day,
And some men were planting potatoes
    In a garden across the way.

So she ran right over to watch them.
    She very much wanted to know
The way that all things must be planted,
    And what's needed to make them grow.

They cut potatoes into pieces,
    But on each piece must leave an eye;
For they never would grow without it,
    But remain in the ground and die.

"Well, I'm sure," said dear little Edith,
    "The eye must help them *see to grow!*
For they never could do without it,
    And my grandpa just told me so."

The Bees

One warm day in Spring, the sun shone right into a beehive that stood under an apple tree in the orchard, and had been the home of the "Brownies" all the long Winter.

The Brownies had worked very hard the Summer before, laying up food for themselves, and for people, too.

They were not lazy or selfish, and never stopped when they had had enough to eat; but went right on, filling their little hexagonal cells, and sealing each one over when it was filled, *just* as your mama seals her can of fruit when it is filled and ready to be put away for the Winter.

When Winter time came, they rested in their home, the hive, until a little Spring sunbeam whispered: "Dear little Brownies, waken from your long nap, and come out into the beautiful world, where the flowers are waiting to welcome you."

Roused from their sleep, they looked about, stretched their legs and wings, and

soon one ventured out, and then another
and another, going to the roof of their little home.

Here they waited, that they all might
go on a journey to the apple blossoms.
Soon they started.

The first trip was a short one, but they
carefully filled their tiny baskets and
started for home.

The next day they were much stronger,
and stood their journey better, flying from
flower to flower in the garden, and away
out in the fields of clover, gathering the
sweet honey.

At night, they came back very tired, but
had plenty of sweet food, which they
stowed away in the queer little cells or
boxes which they had made.

They also gathered the yellow flower
dust or pollen, which they packed away in
the baskets on their legs; and carried it to
the hive to be mixed with honey and be
made into "bee-bread" for the baby bees.

The babies could not thrive without this
bread.

When a bee goes into a flower, it is covered with the yellow flower dust, or pollen;

and the first thing it does, is to brush it off, just as you would brush the dust off from your clothes; only the bee is careful to brush the yellow dust down with little brushes which it has on its legs for that purpose; next he packs it in the baskets as carefully as if it were gold.

. The children, playing in the orchard every day, watched these little Brownies, but they called them "Bees," and when they heard them singing about their work, said: "The bees are humming."

"Then the Brownies laughed in their own way, saying: "We must work and make honey, that the dear little girls and boys may have plenty to eat."

When the weather grew cold, the Brownies had earned their rest, and had plenty of food laid up in their homes.

Little Brown Bees

Dear little brown bees, always busy,
  Pray tell, do you ever sigh,
When you think of the work you're doing?
  Does it make you tired to fly?

When among the sweet clover blossoms,
　Gathering the honey dew,
Do you think of the good you're doing
　As you sing the whole day through?

"Oh, fairest little maiden, ever,
　When amid the flowers we roam,
Of the dear little folks we're dreaming,
　As we fill our honey combs.

"We will work enough in the Summer,
　To last us the whole year through.
We will never grow tired or weary,
　For we work, sweet child, for you."

All Is Mine

I was wheeling my baby boy
　Out for the afternoon,
Under some fine catalpa trees
　Which were then all in bloom.

The little darling glanced upward,
　Waving his plump arms white,
While his face with joy was beaming.
　He then cried in delight:

"All is mine! All for the baby!"
  And we were glad to hear
That even this little cherub
  Cared for the flowers so dear.

The trees arched over the sidewalk
  (On each side a row grew),
And over us the floral arch
  Was tossing blossoms new.

Each cluster was full of perfume.
  We paused in great delight,
While the baby boy repeated:
  "All is mine!" and the sight

Pleased a gentleman very old,
  Who was out for a stroll.
He paused, saying: "Darling baby,
  It may seem very droll,

"But there's many older people
  Who've not yet learned, my boy,
That God gives us all these blessings
  That we may them enjoy.

"So we will look around us, as
  'Tis meant for you and me.
Yet many older than you, dear,
  Do not this beauty see."

PART FOUR

SUMMER

Gath'ring Summer Flowers

The Summer Time

JUNE

Birdies giving concerts,
  Roses all a-bloom,
Breezes filled with perfume—
  That's the month of June.

JULY

Shooting off firecrackers,
  Eating good ice cream.
Time flies all too swiftly,
  In July, 'twould seem.

AUGUST

Going out for picnics,
  Gath'ring Summer flowers,
Playing in the meadows
  Through the August hours.

. . . . .

We welcome these three months,
  Full of Summer cheer.
They bring joy and gladness
  To the children dear.

The Pigeons

Tommy had gone out into the country for a few weeks' visit with his grandpa.

Before he had been there many days, he found it was such a wonderful place, and so unlike the city, that he almost thought he would like to stay there all the time.

He climbed the trees and got the apples down, gathered ripe grapes from the vines, and ate the plump peaches which grew on the peach tree.

He was a very good boy, and did not spend all of his time for himself. He took such good care of the chickens that they soon learned to love him. He watered the horses and petted the little calf, until they felt almost as well acquainted with him as if he had always been there.

Tommy had been given a flowerbed to care for, and he spent a great deal of time with his plants.

One day, when he was pulling weeds, and digging around the plants, he heard something flutter down very near him, and turned to see what it could be.

There was the most beautiful pigeon he had ever seen! Such pink little feet, pretty, bright eyes, and lovely grey and white feathers!

What do you think it was doing? Drinking water out of the dish which Tommy had brought out for the plants.

Now, he had often watched the chickens drink, and noticed how they took a little sip of water, and then threw their heads back and let it run down; then took another sip and did the same way, keeping this up until they had had enough.

But the little pigeon did differently. She put her bill down to the dish, and drank just as a horse does, taking what water she wanted without throwing her head back to swallow it.

Tommy sat very still for fear his little visitor might become frightened.

Soon she had finished drinking, and held her head to one side, walking off with such an important air that Tommy could not help laughing.

After a while, she flew up to the pigeon-house on the tall pole, and went in at the cunning little door.

Tommy thought he would like to peep in there, and see what the pigeon's home looked like. So up he went and was well paid for his trouble.

There, in the small room, with its straw carpet, were the old pigeons, taking care of their two little ones.

After that, Tommy often visited their house, and watched his little feathered friends anxiously to see how they grew.

His grandma told him that pigeons, when first hatched, are much weaker than chickens. A young chicken can run around and find its own food about as soon as it is out of its shell; but a pigeon has to be taken care of until nearly grown.

We do not have to feed them, as the parent birds fill their crops with food, and then fly to the nest, taking food from their crop to fill the bills of the young birds.

The mother pigeon lays two eggs, then she and the father bird take turns sitting. She sits on the eggs at night until about ten o'clock in the morning, then he comes and sits on them until evening, when she comes back to the nest, and he goes away for his rest.

Seventeen days after the eggs are laid, the young are hatched. In just four weeks they are quite large and fill the nest, so that there is no room for the parents. They go to another nest and the mother lays two more eggs. They keep this up in Winter and in Summer, thus raising many families of little ones during a year.

They represent the family life more nearly than any other birds as they each select their mate, and live in pairs.

When Tommy went back to the city he told his playmates about the wonderful things he had learned.

Summer Rain

The rain is falling fast!
  I can't go out to play,
But dust on leafy tree
  Will now be washed away.

The farmer is so glad
  To see this gentle rain,
Because it came in time
  To save his crop of grain.

And little boys and girls,
　How happy you should feel,
That God sends sun and rain
　To give you flour and meal!

For these we could not have
　Without his loving care.
Then let us all be glad
　That we so well may fare.

Story of the Snail

Mabel and John lived in a beautiful city, and a few miles from their home was a lovely grove, where trees of all kinds grew, and moss covered the ground.

Many a nice time they spent there, gathering ferns and flowers, or if in the Autumn, searching for the walnuts, hazelnuts, butternuts, and hickory nuts to be put away for Winter.

One day they started for the grove, taking a nice lunch which their mother had packed in a basket, for they intended staying several hours.

As the carriage was a two-seated one, mother and Aunt May accompanied them.

They gathered many wild flowers and got some very tall ferns to press; but the most curious thing they found was a little snail, which Mabel picked up.

She did not even know what it was, for it was the first one she had ever found. Aunt May told her this story about it.

"Mr. Snail has no particular home, but travels around, and, like a soldier, takes his tent with him. We might call the snail's shell a tent or house, for he carries it on his back and goes into it at night.

"These snails are hatched from tiny white eggs. When they come out, they eat the egg shell, and start out to get some food.

"They begin to take care of themselves at once, and always know what is best for them.

"The queerest thing is, that as they grow larger, the house keeps growing too, so they have the same house when full grown that they had when hatched.

"Their bodies are flat on the under sides, and instead of feet, are provided with a great number of little suckers to hold on to the stones or wood over which they creep. They never go around such objects, but always over them.

"Their shells are striped with brown and gold while they are living, but after they die the shell turns white.

"As they can not run or go very fast, we often hear the expression: '*As slow as a snail.*'

"Now," said Aunt May, "I must tell you about their heads, which are short and provided with four horns. The upper pair are the larger and on the tips are tiny black specks supposed to be eyes. When any one touches a snail he draws his horns in.

"They lay their eggs just underneath the surface of the soil.

"The thrush is a great killer of snails, and pays for the fruit he eats by destroying them, for they are the gardeners' enemies.

"In Winter they go into seclusion, closing the opening to their shell home, with a layer of hardened mucus, sometimes strengthened by the same substance of which their shell is composed; and always perforated with a tiny hole, to admit air so they can breathe."

When you are playing the snail game at kindergarten, you will think of the story your auntie has told you, and also of the little pet we found today.

The Three Fishes

It was a great tank at the World's Fair in Chicago.

Many, many fishes, large and small, ugly and pretty, dark and light, had been placed there for exhibition; for throngs of people came from all over the world to see the sights.

One little boy who went there with his parents, declared that he not only *saw* all of those wonderful fishes, but heard some of them talk.

His mother told him that since fishes can not talk, he must have had a dream about them; but he stoutly declared that they really did tell him a story about themselves.

"There were three fishes," he said, "talking very loudly, and each thought himself the finest fish.

"Finally the largest one said: 'We will leave it to this little boy as to who is the nicest.'"

William, for that was the boy's name, disliked telling which one he really liked the most, so he said, "You are all very nice, and I wish I could take you home with me; but as I have no right to do that, I hope one of you will tell me all about *fishes,* for I want to learn about them;" and he declares that the goldfish, who was very tame, and fond of children, began the following story:

"We live in the water, as you see. We could not live on the land if we should try, for we are made to swim, and live in water.

"We do not wear feathers, like the birds, fur like cats, squirrels and many other animals, nor hair like the horse and dog; but we are dressed in *scales.*

"The scales with which most fish are covered, are beautiful, and increase in size according to the age of the fish. They are attached to the skin by *one edge* and overlap each other in such a way as to allow us to pass easily through the water.

"When we want to move rapidly we give repeated strokes of our muscular tails. Our fins are employed as balancers, and sometimes to check onward motion.

"We are sub-aqueous, which means, unfit for life on dry land. Our gills are so constructed that they can furnish sufficient oxygen for the aeration of the blood.

"If gold fish are kept in too small a supply of water, or the vessel is small at the mouth, so as to keep out a plentiful supply of air, the fish come gasping to the top, and with mouths wide open, eagerly gulp in the air.

"The reason fishes die when taken from the water, is that the delicate gill membranes become dry and close against each other. Thus the circulation of blood is stopped, and the oxygen of the air can no longer act upon it.

"Fishes have cold blood and their hearts are simply constructed.

"Some cannot hear, but many species are capable of hearing sounds, and carp can be taught to come for their food at the blowing of a whistle.

"Our sense of touch is located chiefly in the mouth, or near it, and our eyes are covered with a transparent skin, which keeps out the water.

"I have told you all I can think of now about the fishes. You ask how I know all of this? For a long time I was kept in a globe on a teacher's desk, and could not help but hear the lessons about fishes as she repeated them to her pupils. Good-by for this time, little boy, said the gold fish."

The Fishes

As I sit by the water so clear,
  By the side of the beautiful brook,
There comes, gliding dangerously near,
  A fish. Ah! he has just missed my hook!

Well done, little fish, may you ever
  In your freedom, the clear waters roam.
In the world, there's nothing so clever,
  As you dears in your watery home.

Clover Blossom Borders

Mama was sitting on the porch, reading.

Presently the children came up with their arms and aprons full of pretty red clover blossoms.

One little tot began placing hers on the porch floor thus:

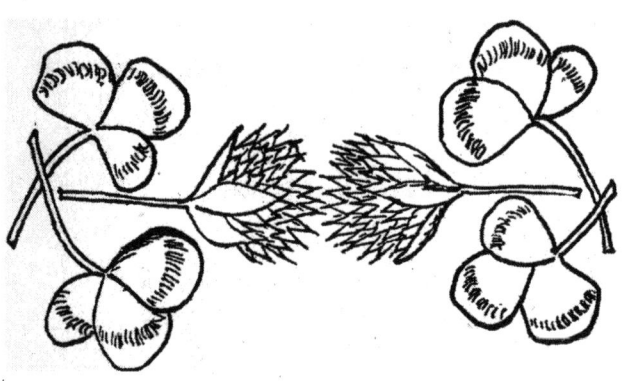

Immediately all the children placed theirs in some pretty way to form a border.

Mama said, "What lovely borders!" All try to see what pretty ones you can make, and to the one having the best, I will give a prize.

One little girl made a border by repeating the design with clover leaves and blossoms.

Some day you try to make borders with flowers and leaves, and see what you can do.

The Swing

Fasten the rope to the limb so strong,
  Of the dear old apple tree.
There in leafy shade, we children all
  Can now swing quite merrily.

The little birds are musicians, gay;
  The sky is our roof of blue!
We will sing and join their roundelay,
  Floating o'er our carpet new

With soft grassy carpets neath our feet,
  Let us swing up high—high—high.
We catch the leaves of the fine old tree,
  As we travel toward the sky!

Little Bird, Tell Me

Little bird, why can't you stop
  And talk to me?
Tell me why you build your nest
  Up in a tree?

Tell me why you're never still,
  And why you get
Your dinner from the garden,
  My little pet?

Do the worms taste good to you?
    And do you know
Where for seeds and cherries good
    A bird should go?

For your quarters in my tree
    You pay the rent,
With the blithesome songs you sing
    Which, too, are sent,

As praises to Him on high
    Who gave to you
Your sweet little music box
    And coat of blue.

Then build your nest in my tree,
    And come again!
Of the cherries, help yourself,
    And taste the grain.

If you take my cherries ripe,
    I will not care.
With your songs you pay for them,
    Oh, bird so rare!

The Spider and His Ways

Spiders are often called "insects," but they are not. The spider has eight legs, whereas an insect cannot have more than six.

The circulation, respiration and nervous system are constructed on an entirely different principle.

Their eyes are also different, the insects having many compound eyes, and spiders never more than eight, of simple construction.

The spider has no separate head, as in the case of insects, the head and thorax being fused together.

Another difference is, spiders do not pass through a series of developments which we call "transformations."

It is hatched out a *spider* and retains the same shape through life.

No insect can spin silken threads. Let us refer to the silkworm. The silk is spun by the caterpillar and not by the moth

Now, the spider, throughout its whole life, can spin threads, and has the power to spin different kinds of silk, according to the object for which it is needed.

They consume quantities of flies, although we do not miss many. It is estimated that a spider eats six or seven times its own weight in a single day.

Some people consider them repulsive, but God has made them very useful and given them great beauty of their own.

Never can one find anything so tiny possessing such wonderful skill.

If a bee, wasp or anything too large for him to attack, gets into his web, he wisely sets it free.

Some have beautiful skin, spotted with orange or yellow, and when this skin gets dull and old, he throws it off for a fresh coat. He gets a new set of legs quite often, and if any accident happens, causing the loss of a leg, it soon grows out again. This is also true of lobsters and crabs.

At the ends of the spider's legs are claws, and he has two short forearms that enable him to firmly sieze his prey.

He can drop himself down by a silken

thread, and then run up to his web again, very quickly. By the same strand, he can swing in all directions.

His senses are very acute. He can tell what the weather is to be, and always knows when a storm or frost is coming, and leaves his web, for snug shelter in his nest.

So we see, they are really very wonderful, and can do something besides crawl.

From these little spiders we learn the lessons of industry, accuracy of work in all of its details, and patience. It is said a spider will reconstruct its web as often as it becomes destroyed, never giving up.

This reminds us of the poem, "Try Again," which used to be a part of our school readers.

Try Again

'Tis a lesson you should heed—
    Try again;
If at first you don't succeed,
    Try again;
Let your courage then appear,
For, if you will *persevere,*
You will conquer, never fear;
    Try again.

Once or twice though you should fail,
    Try again;
If you would at last prevail,
    Try again;
If we strive, 'tis no disgrace,
Though we do not win the race.
What should we do in that case?
    Try again.

If you find your task is hard,
    Try again;
Time will bring you your reward;
    Try again;
All that other folks can do,
Why, with patience, may not you?
Only keep this rule in view—
    Try again.

Robert Bruce and the Spider

Way over in Scotland, there lived a man named Robert Bruce.

He did many brave deeds, and was so good and persevering that I wish every little boy and girl could know about him, and grow to be as persevering as he was.

Scotland was ruled by England, and while Robert Bruce's grandfather and father both had a right to the throne, they gave it up, and swore allegiance to England's King, rather than fight for their rights.

But Robert felt that he should rightfully be the King of Scotland, as the crown had been worn by his ancestors. Therefore he tried to free his country from England.

Six battles were fought and lost, and he became discouraged.

Who would not be discouraged and lose heart after six hard battles, and not a victory won?

After the sixth battle, sad and disheartened, Robert Bruce lay down in a hut to rest. As he was lying in the rude hut in the forest, trying to determine whether to *try again* for the seventh time, he looked up and saw a tiny spider, trying to fix its web on the rafters, and was swinging itself from one beam to another.

The King was amused by the patience and energy displayed by the tiny little spider.

It had tried *six times* to reach one place, and failed.

Suddenly the thought struck the Scottish monarch: "I have fought six times against the enemies of my country."

He decided to be guided by the failures or successes of this little spider.

The next effort of the spider *was successful;* so Robert Bruce decided to make the seventh attempt to free his country, now feeling sure he would yet achieve the liberty of Scotland.

No wonder he was such a success in his undertaking, for the lesson of perseverance learned from the tiny spinner, prompted him to go on, and at last the victory was his.

The Conquered Lesson

"Oh, dear! I'm so very tired;"
  Said little Ben, one day.
"I've tried to get my lesson,
  But now I want to play."

"And yet this old example
  I can not seem to do.
I think I will give it up,
  And go and play with you."

"But work should always come first,"
    The teachers do relate,
"So I'll go and try again.
    Perhaps I'll change my fate."

And sure enough, he quickly,
  By trying hard once more,
Soon got the correct answer,
  And scampered out the door.

Let us always try again,
  If lesson hard doth seem.
Do you really want to conquer?
  Then put on lots of steam.

Getting Rid of the Sweet Peas

Aunt Susie was a lover of flowers, and the yard around her house was full of beautiful blossoms, old fashioned ones, and new varieties.

The roses were so numerous and beautiful that the place was called "Rose Bower."

Her sweet peas were her delight, and when I came to visit her, she said, "Well, I am glad to have my niece here to help me care for my sweet peas.

"They must be cut every day, so as not to allow them to go to seed, and as there are so many, can be sent to the poor, or the sick."

So every evening she went out with her shears and clipped the slender stems. Then she sent great bunches of them to the minister, to an old lady who had no flowers, and sometimes to the sick.

One evening, she had a great many, and could think of no one to give them to. I

suggestea tne minister, but she had just
sent him a cartload yesterday.

"Then give them to the *sick*," I said.
But she knew of no one who was sick.

At last, she started me out, saying, "Do
go and find some one to give these sweet
peas to."

"But to *whom* shall I give them?" I inquired. "You might stop at Mrs. Jerold's
with them," she replied.

Accordingly, I started, carrying a huge
bunch of the blossoms. as large as a great
cabbage.

Soon I came to Mrs. Jerold's house, and
rang the bell. There was no one at home,
and I was glad of it, for as I turned to
leave, I saw a long row of sweet peas near
the alley fence, and what *would* she have
thought if I had offered them to her?

I walked on, not daring to take the flowers back, and being a determined person,
disliked giving up. So I strolled toward
Mrs. Gilcrest's, only to find that she, too,
had sweet peas.

No matter which way I went, all the
neighbors had them. They seemed to be
contagious.

I finally offered them to a *cow* who was grazing near a fence, but she refused them, and gave a big *snort*.

It was now getting dusky, and I felt that I must turn toward home.

I was sure that all who met me could read in my face that I was quite bothered over the fact that I could not get rid of my sweet peas.

Finally, I saw ahead of me, in the board walk, a friendly knothole—generous and large! Into it I stuck the stems of my bunch of sweet peas! Home I turned, free and happy again! But imagine Aunt Susie's surprise.

"Well," I said, "I have a 'get-rich-quick scheme.' Just let your sweet peas go to seed, then sell the seed, for which there seems to be great demand, since most everyone is raising them!"

But if we want to give flowers away, lets send to South America, or some place far off, and get some seeds of a *new flower* that none of them have ever seen."

The next Summer we did so; and then
they all came and begged our seeds.
But we said:
   "If you plant our seeds,
   They'll be common as weeds."
None, therefore, would we give them.

The Dandelion

A wise mother fairy
   Lives over the hill.
She wears fine green dresses
   With many a frill.

Her children are many,
   And to her are true.
I'm sure their bright faces
   Would surely please you.

In bright yellow dresses
   The color of gold,
They gorgeously flourish
   Like monarchs of old.

Her dear eldest children
   Are helpers, you see,
And little white jackets
   They send o'er the lea.

Some fields are quite golden
    So many are there;
And some people love them,
    While others just stare

And call them "a nuisance
    To choke out the grass;"
So they hire, to dig them,
    Both laddie and lass.

But dear little children
    Their firm friends will be,
And pick them for teachers
    Who are pleased, as we see;

'And put them in vases
    Upon their school desks;
So you see, not by all
    They're thought of as pests.

Besides their bright colors
    To make the world gay,
Their long stems furnish curls
    For children at play.

Thus all things in Nature
    Will give us pleasure,
If we their real beauty
    Our minds can measure.

Studying in the Woods

"Children, I think we would all like to take a walk in the woods today," said Uncle George.

"It is a lovely Summer day, and we will take some lunch along, so we need not hurry home.

"There is so much to see and so much to learn."

"What will we learn about this time?" inquired Willie.

"I will tell you a good plan," replied uncle, "we will study about just whatever you children happen to see first.

"All of you keep your eyes open, and we will see what it shall be."

So two little boys, Albert and Willie, and their two sisters, Ellen and Dorothy, went to the grove with their uncle.

As they came near the leafy forest trees, Albert saw a frisky squirrel trying to hide among the foliage of a great oak, and he thought they should learn about the squirrels.

So they all sat down in a shady place, while Uncle George told them a story.

He said: "Now sit quite still for I do not like to tell a story to children who are not paying attention.

"The squirrel is quite richly dressed in fur, as we see. He has a bushy tail, bright eyes, and is very sprightly.

"He is admired a great deal by animal lovers.

"Many a boy is ambitious to have a pet squirrel, and in cities, there are men who catch these little animals, and sell them. Some of them are great cheats, and will tell that the squirrel is very tame, and put their fingers in his mouth to prove it, but this seeming tameness is caused by a dose of strychnine, which has made the little animal dull and lifeless."

"How mean to treat the poor little thing like that!" exclaimed both boys together. "Yes," said uncle, "and the purchaser would have been greatly cheated, for the squirrel would only live a few hours.

"Sometimes they have an old squirrel to sell, and to pass it off as a gentle, young one, they pull out its front teeth, and show

how it does not bite your finger. Being dependent on these strong, chisel-shaped teeth for the preparation of their food, they soon die.

"The age of the squirrel is told by the teeth. If he is young, the teeth are quite white; but when old, they are of a deep yellow."

"What is the best way to get a pet squirrel?" inquired Willie.

"It is best to take the little fellow from the nest yourself," replied uncle.

"One should try to select him about the middle of Summer.

'If taken when quite young they are easily tamed, and will show no fear of their little master.

"I once knew a boy who had a fine pet squirrel. It would play with him, and perch on his head, take nuts from his pockets, and crack them, and was very happy.

"But they are not so happy with all boys. It depends upon the boy," said uncle. "If you ever have a pet, I hope you will be kind to him, keep his cage clean, and give him all the food and water he needs. They

must have nuts, acorns, etc., as the struc-
ture of their teeth is such as to compel them
to be constantly nibbling."

"I think I will get a squirrel sometime,"
said Albert, "and I mean to be kind to him
if I do."

"I have know of these little pets refusing to leave their owners, preferring to
live in captivity, and refusing to return to
the grove when set free. They certainly
learn to appreciate human kindness.

"Now let us walk along, for we are tired
of sitting."

As they strolled along, little Dorothy
told them about a squirrel that she once
saw at her kindergarten.

She said: "We were going to learn a
song about the squirrel, and so Miss Clara
told the boys to bring a real live one for us
to look at, and learn about.

"The very next morning a lady came in
her automobile, bringing a fine new squirrel cage and a lovely young squirrel was
in it. It belonged to her little boy.

"As Miss Clara was taking him out of
the cage, he got away and ran around the
room. This made the children laugh, and

he thought he would hide, so he ran right
into the piano. It was a large old fashioned piano like grandma's" said Dorothy.
"The teacher had quite a time getting him
out, and after that, he was kept in his cage.

"After a few days, he was sent home,
for there was danger of his being killed
with kindness, as the children all loved him,
and fed him more than he should eat. He
never lacked for nuts and good things."

"Look at that ant!" cried Ellen. "He is
carrying a crumb of bread or something.
It is many times larger than he is." They
all stopped to watch the tiny insect. He
was making a great effort to take his prize
home, but soon he became quite exhausted,
and ran around, looking at it from all sides,
as if trying to find a better place to take
hold. At last he started off to the ant hill
to get help. He seemed to make some of
the ants know what he wanted, and back
he started, followed by several little helpers. They took hold with him, and succeeded in carrying their prize to the ant
hill.

Arriving there, some went into the door
of their home, and pulled the crumb down,

while others pushed, until they succeeded
in getting it where they wanted it."

"Is not that a lesson of perseverance?"
said Uncle George. "Even the tiniest of
us are capable of doing a great deal, and
can help others to accomplish what they
wish to do.

"The Bible says:
Go to the ant, thou sluggard: consider her ways, and be wise:
Which, having no guide, overseer
or ruler,
Provideth her meat in the Summer,
and gathereth her food in the harvest.

"Now we will sit here and eat our lunch,
where we can watch our insect friends.
They certainly teach us great lessons of industry and patience."

Then Willie startled them by saying:
"I don't think these little ants are much
good. They got into our sugar once, and
mama had a great time getting rid of
them." "I once put some candy away in a
box," said Dorothy, "and when I went to
get it, the ants were there, enjoying a great
treat, and I had to throw it all away."

"That is true," their uncle replied.

"They really are troublesome and destructive little insects.

"In South America they travel in what might be called small armies, and destroy telegraph and telephone poles if made of wood; therefore, they have to make them of iron.

"Even new lumber has been spoiled by them, and rendered unfit for building purposes."

Just then they were joined by little John, who had some English walnuts, which he passed to them. While they were eating the walnuts, he said:

*I am a little walnut,
  The little fairy dear;
And sometimes people crack me,
  And then sweet meats appear.

When I'm cracked and shelled for them,
  And ready for their food,
Then they quickly taste of me,
  And cry: 'Oh, my! how good!'

The children all clapped their hands and laughed. "You learned that from your

*A true incident, known to the author.

school reader, I suppose?" his uncle re-
marked. "No," said little John. "I just
made it up while we were eating these good
nuts." "Pretty good for a little boy only
nine years old!" they all cried.

As it was time to return to their home,
they left the pleasant grove, declaring that
they would come back often for more lessons.

A Boy's Toy Store

"I've a new toy store," said little Ben,
    Right under the apple tree.
An old pine box is my long counter,
    Full of toys for you to see.

"There Billiken Doll, with his odd smile,
    Sits close to a Teddy Bear;
And Baby Bumps, the dear little thing,
    Is awake. Just see her stare!

"There are dollies' tea sets, trimmed in
        gold,
    There are chairs and tables, too.
If you're sure you have *money* enough,
    I'll sell some of them to you.

"Stretched across two flat stones, there's a
board,
   And it's full of toys for boys.
I can show you whistles, tops, or drums,
   If you wish to make a noise."

The children marched up with pocketbooks,
   And bought the toys they wanted;
Thus Ben's store quickly came to an end,
   Sooner than he had counted.

Sponges

All of the sponges utilized in commerce
belong to the genus spongia. Six species
are now known and these each have many
varieties.

Three species are found in the Mediter-
ranean and Red seas, and three belong to
the Bahamas and Florida Reef.

The sponges which we find on our coasts
are coarse, yet are used a great deal in
housework.

Just the minute sponges are taken out of
the water, they die.

They are said by many to belong to the

animal kingdom and if they do they form the lowest link in the animal chain.

Since their whole surfaces are filled with holes of various sizes, the name "porifera" is given to them.

Sponges grow upon almost every solid body to be found in the seas, and when alive, their colors are many and beautiful.

The living sponge is of a gelatinous texture, and if we view it under the microscope, we see separate bodies, which are supplied with long cilia. The cilia dash the water away, scatter the solid particles, but retain those which are useful in digestion.

They have a fibrous network which serves as a support to them. When fastened to rocks, their growth is in a regular process.

To free them from the jelly-like animal matter of which they consist when first bought, they are buried in sand, where they are kept a few days. They are then put to soak, and finally washed.

In the sponge fisheries of Turkey the sponge is secured by diving.

The best sponges are found from eight

to ten fathoms below the surface of the water.

On the Bahama Islands, a pronged fork is used to detach the sponges from the rocks.

A Nature Lover

What are you doing, dear little Beth,
    Out there by my cherry tree?
"I'm hanging cabbages on the limbs,
    For little papoosies," said she.

"Those Indian squaws in picture books,
    Their little papoosies would hang
On boughs of trees when they went to call;
    And winds rocked as little birds sang."

What are you doing, dear little Beth,
    Standing on that box so high?
"Why, these Autumn leaves are dollie's clothes
    That I'm pinning up to dry."

So she pinned each leaf to mama's line
    With her mama's real clothespins;
Thus showing us by her childish play,
    How 'tis Nature's heart she wins

What are the things you are selling here—
  In your toy store large and new?
"'Tis candy made from maple leaf stems,
  Tied up in bunches for you."

So all day long the little child plays
  While Nature furnishes toys,
Showing that if we have minds to see,
  There's much in our girls and boys.

   This poem was suggested by actual observation of a
child at play.—AUTHOR.

Our Pet Dogs

Dogs are carnivorous, or flesh eating animals. Although they belong to this class, they can subsist on vegetable food, and are very fond of bread or biscuit.

A hungry dog will eat almost any food he can get, not having as dainty an appetite as the cat.

Dogs are great favorites with many people, because they are so intelligent, and show much love for their owners.

They seem to know at once if they are welcome, and express marked appreciation for everything done for them.

If they have had the proper training from the beginning, they know at once if they have done wrong or have offended you.

They will hide under a table or some other piece of furniture, and refuse to come out until their master has first spoken some encouraging word of forgiveness.

A dog who minds from fear will look up to his master with a frightened expression, and appear afraid of him at all times.

It is best to use gentle firmness from the first, and never the whip.

The poodle, the terrier, and the spaniel are great favorites for pets.

The Newfoundland dog is very intelligent, and shows great love for children who play with him.

At one time, a little child was playing on a wharf with his father's Newfoundland dog, when he accidentally fell into the water. The faithful dog quickly leaped in after him, and taking hold of the child's dress, swam to the dock, where he could hold on to the platform. When he saw that the little fellow could not pull himself out, and that his own efforts also failed to lift him from the water, he ran to a yard near by, where he saw a girl.

He took hold of her dress, and almost dragged her to the spot. She at once started to lift the child out, and the brave dog did all he could to assist her.

When he saw that the little boy was safe, he went back into the stream and found the child's hat, which he brought to him.

These noble dogs are so brave that they will go into a burning building to save a life.

A friend of mine once had a faithful shepherd dog who would bring the paper into the house every day. He would drive the cows home, and if the gate was shut, would bark until some one opened it for him.

About the house he made himself useful, caring for the children when they were

at play. At night he was a faithful watch
dog.

Many of you have seen Bronte, the wonderful dog who knows so much, for he has
been shown in a great many cities in the
United States.

He can look at a passing car and tell the
number of it. Once a car came along having the number forty-two on the front in
large figures.

His owner asked him "What number
was on the car?" He gave four barks, then
two more, to indicate forty-two.

You may think this was all the arith-
metic he knew; but he could tell how many
two and two were, or three and three. ·

Once he was asked the number of buttons on a little boy's coat. He gave six
sharp barks to indicate "six," which was
correct

There are many things more that he
could do, but there is not space to tell them
here.

No doubt my little readers have dogs of
their own, who can perform many tricks.

Some of them, I am sure, can shake

hands, sit up on their hind feet, and beg, or jump through a hoop.

The first thing a child does when he gets a dog, is to try to find some suitable name for his pet. A black dog is often called "Nig" or "Beauty." A large dog often goes by the name of "Hero," if he is noted for brave deeds.

Many little pets I have seen, answered to the names of "Curly," "Fluffy," and "Snowball," while one little dog who is often in mischief, is known as "Buster."

We should be kind to all of our little animal friends, that they may have confidence in us and love us.

Never forget to feed and water them every day, for they depend upon you for this care.

The Child's Question

Are the stars the moon's children
  As she travels so high?
And what work is she doing
  In her home in the sky?

I have heard that she borrows
  Her bright light from the sun.
As she sails through the cloudland,
  Does she please every one?

The Mother's Answer

It may seem to the children
  The moon's nothing to do.
She influences the tides,
  As I'll explain to you.

Tides resemble great waves, and
  Raised by her attraction,
Follow her course round the earth
  Much to her distraction.

The sun, too, causes the tides,
  But the moon is nearer;
Thus she has greater effect
  On the watery mirror.

The tides are twelve hours apart,
  And come twice every day.
The law of gravitation
  Clearly's shown in this way.

Now, my dear little children,
  Keep your eyes open wide
There is much to be learning
  As you're watching the tide.

Our Shoes

Have you ever visited a shoe factory in one of our large cities?

If you have not, you have missed a great deal.

A long time ago, the cobbler used to sit and work with his leather and waxed ends, doing everything by hand, and turning out only one pair of shoes a day.

Now, our shoes are made by machinery, and each operator turns out about five pairs of shoes a day.

I once visited a large shoe factory in St. Louis. The first room we entered was the cutting room, where the upper parts of shoes were cut out, then stitched and eyeleted by machinery.

With just one motion the eyelet machine punched the holes on both sides and put in all the eyelets. They were then sent into another room, where the bottom pieces and heels were cut of sole leather by machinery.

They were then passed to the bottoming room, where inner and outer soles were fastened temporarily to the uppers.

The heel is then nailed on, and the sole permanently stitched or nailed and the edges trimmed off. In the finishing room, the edges of the soles and heels are stained.

We then visited the treeing room, where the uppers were oiled and polished.

The shoes were then placed in pairs, wrapped in soft paper and packed in their proper boxes, ready to be sent to the stores.

In the West, St. Louis ranks first in the manufacture of shoes, Milwaukee second, and Chicago third. Very few of the shoes from these factories are exported, but are sold in the middle West. The Eastern and New England States export over six million pairs each year.

Machinery for the manufacture of shoes was first invented and used in the United States, and is now being introduced into Europe.

For a long time, shoes were made alike for both feet; but in the nineteenth century lefts and rights were thought of, and the result was more comfortable and better looking shoes.

In another lesson we will learn about the leather of which our shoes are made.

Leather

Where do you think we get the leather from which our shoes are made?

It is made from the skins of animals, which are tanned.

By accident, a great many years ago, the discovery was made that hemlock bark acted upon the gelatine in the fibers of the skin, changing them into tough substances. So they took the skins of animals and changed them to leather by this process, called "tanning."

The place where this is done is called a tan yard or tannery.

Many hides are sent to the tannery, where they are packed in salt to preserve them.

They are then soaked in water several days, and washed.

Strong lime water is then prepared, and they are soaked in this a few more days, to loosen the hair, which is removed.

Hemlock bark, ground fine, is steeped, and in this liquor the hides are soaked.

Sometimes hides are put into vats, and layers of bark placed among them, which help the solution to produce the chemical action on the skins and hides.

Heavier leather, of which heels and soles of shoes are made, comes from the backs and shoulders of cattle, and some of it comes from the buffalo. Heavy leather requires a longer time for tanning.

The lighter weight, finer skins, of which the upper parts of shoes are usually made, comes from the hides of calves, goats and sheep.

Morocco comes from hides of sheep and goats, and is used for binding books.

Leather used for belts, bags, gloves and pocketbooks, is called Shamoyed leather.

This is a fine, soft leather, produced by combining the gelatin with oils and fatty substances.

When you are in the stores, you see a great many articles made of leather, do you not?

No doubt, you could name, or write a long list of uses for leather.

Milk, Butter and Cheese

A little girl friend of mine had lived in a large city all of her life and did not know how a cow looked or what a cow was.

The milk her mama used was condensed milk, bought at the grocery, and put up in cans; or, sometimes, milk bought from the milkman's wagon.

One day she was made very happy by being taken to the country to see her uncle, who owned a fine farm.

There she saw the men milking the cows, and when they went to the house with their large full pails of milk, it was to her, a great sight.

She had all the rich milk she could drink, and enjoyed the sweet, fresh country butter on her bread. As strawberries were ripe, she ate them with the rich Jersey cream and sugar. Do you not think she grew strong and rosy?

When she went back to the city her friends hardly knew her.

Another little girl who was a great friend of hers, did not use milk and cream.

When strawberries were given to her, she said, "I'll take my strawberries bare," meaning that she did not like them with sugar and cream.

She was not as strong and rosy as the other child, for milk contains properties to be found in the blood and is what children need to build them up. All children should try to like the nice milk, cheese and butter.

Some butter is made on the farms, but a great deal is now made at creameries, by machinery which is operated by electricity or steam power.

In the creamery, a large quantity, sometimes over a hogshead of cream, is made into butter at one time; then it is worked by machinery, and packed into casks for the markets.

Some of it is made into one pound bricks, and carefully wrapped, so no hands touch it until it reaches the consumer. It is thus away from all dust and odors of the grocery, which penetrate butter if exposed.

A great deal of cheese is also made at the factories. It is largely composed of casein and fat, the other properties of the milk passing off into the whey or watery liquid, which is fed to the stock. Some cheese is very rich, because it contains a great deal of fat.

To make cheese, the milk is curdled, by putting in a piece of rennet. Rennet is a piece of a calf's stomach, which acts upon the properties of the milk, making it curdle. The whey is then pressed out, leaving a solid substance, known as the "curd." This is salted, and pressed until no water is left in it, then put away to harden still more, or "ripen into cheese," as it is called.

Nearly all of the cheese now made comes from the factories.

On ships, where fresh milk cannot be had daily, condensed milk is used.

A great deal of this milk is exported, and in large cities it is much used. A great quantity of fresh milk is sold in the large cities, and some of it comes from a long distance, being sent in milk trains.

Every railroad entering New York or Chicago has special milk trains, many having refrigerator cars. I have seen these cars loaded, ready to be sent to New York.

The cans are quite large, holding from five to ten gallons each.

After the milk is received, it is put into bottles, quarts and pints, and sealed ready to be delivered.

Some time ago, milk was put in pans, and set in the cellar to cool, where it was left several hours, waiting for the cream to rise.

Then all the pans had to be skimmed by hand, with a small skimmer, which could not help but leave small particles of cream.

A machine called a "Separator" has since been invented, and is much used.

This takes cream from the milk very quickly and thoroughly.

There are many other things we get from the cow, besides milk, butter and cheese.

Beefsteaks, and nice juicy roasts we find in the meat markets.

The skins, hoofs and horns are all saved, to be made into something useful

The blood is dried and sold for fertilizer. The hides are made into leather, the bones and horns are used for buttons, combs and handles of brushes and knives. Many other things are made from the particles we would suppose would be valueless.

Can you name some of them?

If You Would Be Healthy

If you would be healthy, rosy and fair,
Throw up your windows and let in fresh
    air.
Let the bright sunshine stream in on the
    floor,
And microbes will flee as never before.

Go to bed early and early arise.
If you do this, you will show that you're
    wise.
The health God has given you, try to keep.
'Tis thus you will have no sickness to reap.

Birds live in the air, yet seldom take cold.
You're so much larger! Can't you be as
    bold?
Some people worry, and are full of care,
Afraid to stay here, afraid to go there;

Afraid to eat this, afraid to eat that,
Afraid to be thin, yet hate to be fat.
Now, of all this worry, what is the use?
Stop it, or else I'm afraid you're a goose.

Where Our Rubbers Come From

When you are putting on your rubbers, do you ever stop to think about where the rubber comes from, of which they are made?

The most of our rubber comes from the Amazon region, where rubber trees grow wild.

The best trees are found in low, flooded ground, or near the large rivers, where the roots drink in a great deal of moisture.

Some of it comes from large rubber vines, as in Africa, where the vines grow on the trees making a dense foliage.

Rubber trees are very hard to cultivate, and have been but little understood until recently.

The slightest change in its surroundings often causes the sap to stop flowing, and the forester frequently kills the trees he is trying to help.

Agriculturists have lately learned more about their cultivation, and large rubber plantations have been started in Mexico and other warm climates.

These should prove a good investment, in time, as the modern inventions bring increased uses for rubber.

A great deal is used for rubber tires of bicycles, automobiles and carriages. So much is used for these that rubber is very scarce compared to what it used to be, and we must pay great prices now for our overshoes and rubbers.

No wonder men go from house to house, buying all the old wornout pairs of rubbers they can get, to be made over into our *new* rubbers, and no wonder our *new rubbers* are worn out after a few days' wear.

After these rubber plantations begin to yield their supply each year, it may be very different, for it is hoped the demand will then be met with the best product obtainable.

But I must tell you how the native of Brazil gets the sap from the rubber tree. He cuts a gash in the bark, with his knife or a hatchet, then fastens a cup to the tree with a piece of clay, to catch the sap, which is as white as milk. He gashes about one hundred trees, then gathers the sap from the cups.

He then builds a fire of palm nuts, dips
a wooden paddle into the sap, then smokes
it in the stream of dense smoke which
passes from the fire, through a clay funnel.

This process makes it become hard and
elastic and the smoke gives it a black color.

Nearly all of our rubber comes from
Para.

Good Night, Dear World

When twilight comes, I love to sit
   By mother's knee, and hear her tell
The stories about what she did
   When she was just a little girl.

Then, when it's dark, oh, very dark,
   My eyes are tired and I must sleep;
So mother takes me to my room
   And soon into my bed I creep.

For quite a while I watch the stars
   Who peep at me, with their bright eyes;
And calmly the old moon looks down,
   As if she were so very wise.

Out in the dark, the fireflies go,
  With lanterns bright, to light their way.
Perhaps they help the owls and bats,
  Who do not get their food by day.

And now, dear world, good night, good
      night,
  For I must grow and sleep and sleep.
Nothing to fear or dread have I
  Knowing that God his child doth keep.

Lightning Source UK Ltd.
Milton Keynes UK
UKHW020630210921
390952UK00007B/525